The Dolphin Dynamic

How to Make a Splash in Today's
Shark-Infested Business Waters

By
Laura L. Laaman

CAREER PRESS
3 Tice Road
P.O. Box 687
Franklin Lakes, NJ 07417
1-800-CAREER-1
201-848-0310 (NJ and outside U.S.)
FAX: 201-848-1727

DIVE is a trademark owned by Laura L. Laaman.

Material on pages 175-176 reproduced with express written permission of Letitia Baldrige, 2339 Massachusetts Avenue NW, Washington, DC 20008.

THE DOLPHIN DYNAMIC
HOW TO MAKE A SPLASH IN TODAY'S SHARK-INFESTED BUSINESS WATERS
ISBN 1-56414-222-1, $22.99
Cover design by Dean Johnson Design, Inc.
Printed in the U.S.A. by Book-mart Press

To order this title by mail, please include price as noted above, $2.50 handling per order, and $1.00 for each book ordered. Send to: Career Press, Inc., 3 Tice Road, P.O. Box 687, Franklin Lakes, NJ 07417.
Or call toll-free 1-800-CAREER-1 (NJ and Canada: 201-848-0310) to order using VISA or MasterCard, or for further information on books from Career Press.

Library of Congress Cataloging-in-Publication Data

Laaman, Laura, 1965-
    The dolphin dynamic : how to make a splash in today's shark-infested business waters / by Laura Laaman.
        p.   cm.
    Includes index.
    ISBN 1-56414-222-1 (hard)
    1. Business communication--Miscellanea. 2. Communication in management--Miscellanea. 3. Dolphins--Behavior--Miscellanea.
I. Title.
HF5718.L33   1996
650.1--dc20   95-39529
                                                                                          CIP

Dedication

To the four men in my life who have inspired my Determination, Instinct, Vision and Enthusiasm:

My father, William Foster Jr.; my husband, Joe Laaman; my son Craig Laaman; and my son Derek Laaman.

Acknowledgments

To my husband, Joe, who has helped me accomplish so many incredible things, including this book. Thank you.

To my very own cheerleader and mentor, Dottie Walters, for providing me with the inspiration and direction to continue and expedite my success. Thank you!

To Lilly Walters for her Determination, Instinct, Vision and Enthusiasm. You are truly a dolphin in today's shark-infested business waters. Thank you for your assistance with this project.

Many thanks to my friends who have dedicated themselves to taking care of dolphins. Thank you for taking your valuable time to provide me with amazing and valuable dolphin knowledge.

To the people at the Dolphin Research Center for their concern and compassion for dolphins. Thank you for the environment to turn my fascination for dolphins into a *passion*.

For your valued input, special thanks to Letitia Baldrige, Tom Hopkins and Anne Mahony.

A special thanks to my team of proofers: Joe Laaman, Mike Chamberlain, Burt Siemens, Nicole Wemett-Mahoney, Kristine Niven and Audrey Lohr.

Thank you to my many professional and personal friends who supported me throughout this project. Your support meant everything. Thank you.

Contents

Introduction: DIVE in!   9

Dynamic One: Determination   19
Average is unacceptable/The brawn-plus-brains approach/Practice
and preparation make perfect/Get the most out of your day/The
importance of a carry-along planning system/Procrastination
sharks!/Remove the clutter from your life!/Deal effectively with
interruptions/Schedule and commit to quiet time/Delegate
often/Use wait times effectively/Turn objections and obstacles into
competitive advantages/Follow-up systems to foster
success/Determined image: what customers see/Smoking, gum and
food/Clothes that create a dynamic image/Manners/Image: business
environment and tools of your trade/Team shirts/Determination is a
can-do attitude/Believe in yourself/Associate with "great-attitude
people"/Don't wait for a great day—create one!/Balancing home and
work ethic/Quiz for the Determined Dynamic/Checklist for the
Determined Dynamic/In conclusion about Determination

Dynamic Two: Instinct   69
Reading silent signals/Observing body language/Using silent
signals to understand others/Working within protected
territories/Match their pace/Exploration: encouraging
signals/Visual exploration/Exploring personality styles/The
Determined personality/The Instinctive personality/The Visionary
personality/The Enthusiastic personality/Involving Instinctives and
Visionaries/Reining in Determineds and Enthusiastics/Adapting
your style to others/Career Profile Assessments/Handwriting
analysis or graphology/Mirroring and modeling/Survey, and you
will succeed!/Instinctive listening and questioning skills/Get the
most from open-ended questions/Addressing and understanding
individual needs/Reading commitment signals/Tips for dealing with
difficult people/Six steps to diffuse emotional encounters/Use your
sonar to hire the right team/Employee discipline: how, when and
why/Terminating an employee/Quiz for the Instinctive
Dynamic/Checklist for the Instinctive Dynamic/In conclusion about
Instinct

Dynamic Three: Vision   **135**

Stationing: a technique for clearer Vision/Vision-station-DIVE!/Shaping your success/Visualization/The power of posting/Goal charts/Bar charts/Activity charts/Star boards/Combining mental and physical possession/Help customers envision themselves sold!/Positive internal talk: the law of expectation/Help your team with profitable contests and incentives/What great minds have said about setting goals/Quiz for the Vision Dynamic/Checklists for the Vision Dynamic/In conclusion about Vision

Dynamic Four: Enthusiasm   **163**

Make your nonverbal message dynamic/Positive body language and your image/Positive gestures for a dynamic image/Gestures to avoid/How to exceed expectations/Create an attention-grabbing greeting/Letitia Baldrige on handshakes/Greetings that translate to "good riddance!"/Compliments: a sure path to dynamic connections/Establishing common ground/Use humor to make dynamic connections/How to cope in an unenthusiastic environment/Can-do vocabulary/Turn dismal responses into dynamic dialogue!/Explore your product for features, advantages, and benefits/When you must address a negative/Communicate Enthusiastically on the phone/Maximize a valuable business asset: your voice/Words and phrases to add Enthusiasm to your speech/Quiz for the Enthusiastic Dynamic/Checklist for the Enthusiastic Dynamic/In conclusion about Enthusiasm

Conclusion: Make a Splash!   **211**

Professional training and speaking   **213**

Dive with the dolphins   **214**

The Dolphin Department   **215**

Suggested Reading   **217**

Index   **219**

Introduction: DIVE in!

Dynamic connections

What is it about dolphins that fascinate humans so much? Why are humans so attracted to dolphins? What is this powerful connection between dolphins and humans? Watch humans at a sea park when they see a dolphin—their eyes light up, they smile. A powerful, dynamic connection has been made. Why? Could it be that dolphins work very hard to communicate? Could it be their perpetual smile and seemingly endless supply of enthusiasm? Could it be their instinctive ability to connect with people around them? *Yes*, to all!!

Through my experience as a top salesperson and business person in numerous industries, I have worked very hard to master many of the skills necessary to be ranked in the top echelon of my field. Amazingly, these same skills for success can also be found in dolphins. Yes, dolphins.

My fascination with dolphins goes back to childhood. Of *all* animals, dolphins seemed the most spectacular in their strength, speed and beauty. Most fascinating was that, somehow, dolphins seem to connect with those around them in an easy and natural manner. I went out of my way to see these magnificant, friendly creatures on television and visit them in aquariums.

As an adult and business professional, finding ways to connect with my customers always has been and continues to be of vital importance to me. Since I found myself on my own at the age of 15, I have been dependent on my sales and communications skills. I became highly effective and very successful because of these skills and began training others for success. As I began to teach others how to use my strategies to be successful in their own business, dolphin analogies always seemed to *dive* right into my seminars!

The Dolphin Dynamic

To continue to enrich my seminars and personal success, I began an intense study of dolphins. Several years ago, I started attending hands-on workshops at the Dolphin Research Center (DRC) in Grassy Key, Florida, where I got in the water with dolphins and studied how these intelligent creatures make such dynamic connections with humans.

I learned a great deal from my experience with the dolphins. And I discovered that the lessons I learned were both fascinating and applicable to the professional success and personal happiness of all of us. My experiences confirmed and enhanced the principles I had previously witnessed and embraced from other highly successful professionals. These traits are:

> Determination,
>
> Instinct,
>
> Vision and
>
> Enthusiasm!

I refer to these as the Dolphin Dynamics! The acronym they create? DIVE! (DIVE is a trademark owned by Laura L. Laaman.)

Determination, Instinct, Vision and Enthusiasm—four equally important ingredients whose synergistic effect has resulted in so many successes in my life in which I can feel pride and accomplishment (not to mention a noticeable monetary gain!). After incorporating these dynamics into my seminars, I discovered that they've brought forth incredible results in companies and individuals nationwide. I have organized the four sections of this book around these four dynamics, enabling you to make a splash in today's shark-infested business waters.

When you use Determination, Instinct, Vision and Enthusiasm and just start moving, the dynamics of this formula will, without fail, pull you toward your goals. The Determination will push you. Your Instinct will help you work with people. The Vision will keep you on track and the Enthusiasm will make the journey more enjoyable—both for you and for those around you.

Dad always showed me...

My father owned a furniture store and worked very hard. He was the reason I have what I would call a good and strong work ethic today. He worked very hard to provide his family with a comfortable life and home. Dad served proudly in World War II as a paratrooper. While serving he was seriously wounded and lost most of one leg. Instead of allowing his misfortune to discount his life, he just worked harder and happier than most.

"A man travels the world over in search of what he needs and returns home to find it."

—George Moore

My earliest memories are of working in the store with Dad. He started me at the bottom. Literally! I worked in the service department, in the basement. Daily I witnessed my father's Determination, Instinct, Vision and Enthusiasm.

When I was 12, my parents separated. My father was given custody of my younger brother Billy and me, even though he was very sick with a rare form of cancer. He fought his illness long and hard. His biggest concern seemed to be hanging in there long enough so that he could give his two young children enough love and guidance to help us through life. He did.

When my father died I was only 15 and my brother Billy was 12. We went to live with our mother, despite her problems with alcoholism. She was the only one available to take care of us.

There were changes in the Social Security benefits that year. Because my father was a veteran, my brother and I were entitled to college tuition assistance if we were in college by the end of the year. There were no stipulations of age. I went to local colleges for entrance exams. I passed! However, shortly after that, my mother and I got into a fight. She said something to the effect, "If you don't like it, you know where the door is." I didn't like it and I did know where the door was and I used it. (I was as stubborn then as I am now.)

I gathered a few things and left. My older brother Mark helped me find an apartment. I remember being alone and hungry my first night in my new apartment. Fortunately, there was a small deli downstairs. I bought a box of Cookie Crisp cereal and a carton of milk. I only had a huge ladle to eat with. Primitive, but I enjoyed it. No one to tell me to eat in the kitchen, or not to eat in front of the TV. As frightened as I was, I didn't want to give up the opportunity of attending college. So, barely 16, I was on my own.

To support myself, I got a job as a waitress. Friends told me about other jobs and soon I had one full-time and two part-time jobs all while handling a 12-hour college course load. I studied, worked and slept. I barely knew what a checking account was and didn't think I could legally have one. I kept my tips and paychecks in coffee cans.

When you DIVE into life, success generates success

My dreams grew as did my abilities to achieve them. Although I was studying to be a lawyer, I had always heard that sales was also a lucrative career. So, while I was studying at college, I decided to test out a career in sales. What business did I know? Furniture! During my first interview at a local furniture store, I was able to drop the names of my father's friends who were renowned reps in the industry.

I got the job. I was off in the world of sales! But there was one slight problem. I didn't have any actual sales experience. On my first day, my manager Ted showed me the layout of the showroom. I told Ted that my previous employers didn't carry waterbeds. (I didn't mention my previous employers actually carried ice cream!) Anyway, I asked him to role-play and show me how he would sell me a waterbed. I tried to memorize everything he said and apply it to the sales of all the merchandise in the store. I also observed the top salespeople, and tried to copy all of their best techniques.

Off I went! Although I was barely old enough to drive, within months I was fighting for the number-one position in the store. Within two years I was breaking national records.

One of the many gifts Dad left with me was the power of goal-setting. I set several goals for myself that I wanted to obtain before I hit 30. They were:

- To become a successful trainer and seminar leader, teaching others the skills of making dynamic connections.
- To start my own family.
- To study dolphins and learn more about their ability to make dynamic connections.
- To write this book.

I was so successful at furniture sales, the owner of one company modeled his training program around my skills. I have built a strong reputation as a trainer and today I train thousands around the world. I have had the magical experience of diving with dolphins several times. My husband, Joe, and I are the proud parents of two wonderful boys, Craig and Derek. I turned 30 a month after finding a publisher for this book. And just wait until you see what I have planned for the next 15 years!

What have I learned from all of this? You need to be strong to survive and thrive in business and in life! Many companies go out of business because the owners or employees are out of touch—or simply don't work hard enough. In contrast, many small companies flourish, gaining customer loyalty and miraculous market share—and outperform bigger companies. Dolphins and the lessons they've taught me continue to play an active role in my professional and personal development. The Dolphin Dynamics of Determination, Instinct, Vision and Enthusiasm continue to strengthen my skills and increase my successes. The dolphin's powerful way of connecting with those around them is a lesson for any professional struggling to not just stay afloat, but to thrive in today's shark-infested business waters.

Connections the dolphin way!

Dolphins are masters of motivation. You should see the way they get people emotionally and verbally involved during such programs as Dolphin Therapy. People are so motivated and mesmerized by the magic of the dolphins they do almost anything to get into the water with them—including speaking their first words after a lifetime of silence.

Dolphin Therapy was developed and continues to be run by Dr. David E. Nathanson, Ph.D., in Florida. To date, Dr. Dave (as he prefers to be called) has conducted more than 10,000 therapy sessions. The goal of Dolphin Therapy is to improve the functioning—cognitive, physical or emotional—of an individual. It is a brilliant program that has taught me a great deal, including to be more appreciative of the wonders in ourselves and in the world around us.

Dolphin Therapy has received international recognition as an alternative therapy program. It has had substantial success with physically and mentally challenged children and adults, increasing their attention and focus. In Dolphin Therapy, the therapist asks the participant to do something that has been difficult or impossible for the individual. When the task is performed properly, the participant is rewarded with time in the water with the dolphins. Some attribute the amazing success of Dolphin Therapy to spiritual forces. Some even say mystical and magical forces are at work. Others believe that dolphins possess a telepathy, a sixth sense that allows them to connect with others including these disabled patients. Whatever the theory, there's no doubt—Dolphin Therapy works with life-changing results.

Look for one more way to get the job done!

Joanne had suffered a spinal cord injury as an adult and wanted to participate in Dolphin Therapy. She had accomplished the goals the therapists had set. Now she was ready for her reward—a *fast* dorsal pull!

A dorsal pull gives you an extraordinary feeling of exhilaration and freedom. Typically, in a dorsal pull, you swim out into the lagoon and a dolphin (sometimes two dolphins) swims up to your side. You grasp on to the dorsal fin (the fin on back of the dolphin) and then the dolphin takes you for a ride.

The trainers explained to Joanne that the dolphin, not the trainers, determines the speed of a dorsal pull. Dolphins are known to go slower with children or timid swimmers and faster with more confident swimmers. Somehow, they seem to judge how confident the participant is and, therefore, how fast he or she should go.

Joanne's enthusiasm was contagious. All the trainers and therapists were ready to help her. Joanne eagerly got into the water. Within a short time everyone was painfully aware that her spinal cord injury made hanging on to the dolphin's dorsal fin tremendously difficult. The trainers gave Natua, the dolphin, permission to leave. There were numerous trainers in the water around Joanne, trying to help. Unfortunately, nothing worked. The therapists were forced to give up.

But a combination of Determination, Instinct, Vision and Enthusiasm are much too powerful to be defeated! Joanne's new friend—Natua—had no intention of giving up. He looked for one more way to get the job done! He came racing over, dodging all the humans who watched him in confusion. He quickly and strategically placed his dorsal fin between Joanne's body and her arm, hooking up with her at the back of her elbow (instead of her hand) and took off—Joanne attached! They say it was one of the fastest dorsal pulls in DRC's history!

Determination, Instinct, Vision and Enthusiasm: four wonderful dynamics that have brought me to an extraordinary place in my life. Those I know who use these seem to have a dynamic personality that is hard to resist. This powerful connection is why I succeed, why dolphins succeed and why you can, too. In this book I will show you how to use these four dolphin dynamics to create a singular dynamic—the Dolphin Dynamic—that will help to shape your professional and personal successes.

Connecting with customers

When you use Determination, Instinct, Vision and Enthusiasm, you will be exceeding your customers' expectations. When you do so, you will have established a connection that your competition cannot break regardless of the business waters you swim in.

The Dolphin Dynamic

You may be saying, "Laura, some of my customers are a bit...uh... challenging." Perfect! You will gain immeasurable experience trying out new strategies to connect with your...challenging customers. Often the gruff and grumpy customers turn out to be the best customers—once you make a connection. This sort of customer will bring you more business and referrals than the "easy" kind—mainly because you were the one who took the time to find a way to connect.

Recently I called on the director of training at a Fortune 500 company. He had already put off two people from my office, but I was Determined to do business with his company. He scheduled the meeting for 9:40 a.m. Not 9:30, not 9:45, but 9:40. So, at 9:40, we went into a cold, dreary, small conference room. He said his office was on the other side of the complex and he didn't want to inconvenience me. What he was really doing was not allowing me to be relaxed in a comfortable office surrounding. He knew this would keep the meeting time to a bare minimum.

When we finally sat down, he drilled me with questions. I smiled, responded with Determination and Enthusiasm and didn't flinch. Strong individuals look for any sign of insecurity. After what seemed to be forever, he said, "Okay, I know all about you, but I don't know why you are here. I get many calls each day to see me and I rarely meet with anyone."

I wanted to jump up and down and say, "Yes! I knew what you were doing. I knew I could make it here, and I did." However, I managed to stay calm, keeping my professional decorum. With full composure I told him I was excited to be meeting with him. Enthusiasm is more magnetic than humility. What I would never have said was, "Thank you so much for taking your valuable time to meet with poor little me." Instead, with excitement in my voice I said, "I am confident our training programs will assist you in improving your already strong sales and management team." (Add to your picture of this my sincere and Enthusiastic smile.) "I just need to get to know your direction and focus so that I will best complement your strategy!" Imagine my smile turning dazzling! Well, I thought it was dazzling at any rate!

After 20 short minutes he had to leave the room for a moment, and as he was leaving he said, "I'll return and answer any final questions you have." Final questions? Maybe I wasn't quite as dazzling as I had thought. I was just getting started. Boy, was this guy good. When he returned he looked as rushed and frustrated as ever. In order to have a true connection, the other person must communicate as well. But this guy was not talking and I didn't have anything else to work with to make the connection. I worked with what I saw and took a risk. I said, "Steve, you look like you are having a rough day," in a kind and concerned way.

"A smooth sea never made a skillful mariner."
—English proverb

"I'm having a rough life!" He told me how frustrated he was in his position, about his world travels, the culture of the company and the maze of bureaucracy. As he talked I was able to finally make the connection with him as a person. Our 90-minute meeting ended with Steve giving me an order and three referrals with phone numbers. His parting words to me were, "If those don't work out, just let me know and I'll be happy to provide you with more." I knew how exhilarated Natua must have felt both before and after he had made his dynamic connection with Joanne.

Don't sit on the dock: DIVE in!

Why did Natua search for a way to connect with Joanne? Why and how do many of us overcome the obstacles that we face?

Dolphins always seem to take a proactive approach to creating the motivation necessary to accomplish their objectives. You won't find them passively floating, waiting for their "customers" to take the lead.

I was observing a Dolphin Therapy session in which Alletta the dolphin was trying to motivate a 5-year-old girl to speak her first word. Dr. Dave was asking the little girl to say Alletta's name, but the girl was unresponsive. Suddenly, Alletta decided to take matters into her own fins and find a way to connect with the child. Alletta started bobbing up and down clicking and squealing, as if cheering the little girl on. At first the child seemed unmoved. But eventually Alletta coaxed her to make a significant effort. To the astonishment of her anxious parents, the girl began to sound out "A-lee-ta!" There wasn't a dry eye on the docks. This was another amazing moment with the dolphins for me.

What is the drive that humans (and dolphins) use to hit their targets? Answer: They DIVE into life instead of sitting on the dock. They use the Dolphin Dynamics of Determination, Instinct, Vision and Enthusiasm!

Our business waters today are filled with many sharks. Whether the sharks you are fighting are mega-sized competitors, internal corporate competition or family business infighting, keep in mind that dolphins are more powerful and more intelligent than sharks. Dolphins are able to perform amazing feats, adapting to their waters when necessary. So are you. Dolphins' most amazing skill, however, is their ability to connect with those around them, even with those much different than themselves—humans!

In the four main sections of this book I will give you specific ideas, strategies and techniques to connect with those around you so you and your business can make an immediate splash in today's shark-infested business waters.

Come DIVE with the dolphins and me!

Dynamic One: Determination

"When your desires are strong enough you will appear to possess superhuman powers to achieve."
—Napoleon Hill, author, *Think & Grow Rich*

In this dynamic you will learn:

- Why having and displaying a strong work ethic will make you and your business more successful.
- Why and how to profit from persistence.
- How to overcome obstacles in any setting.

Dolphins are some of the most powerful, determined yet gentle animals I know. They have the ability to travel in dangerous waters, thriving by either outmaneuvering or outswimming their predators— or taking them head on when necessary. Despite the challenges they face, dolphins ultimately stay on course, whether that course is life-sustaining or enjoyment-oriented.

The core of Determination

Work ethic is the core of Determination. My customers are impressed because they perceive me as being a morning, afternoon and evening person with a seemingly unending supply of energy. Am I a morning, afternoon and evening person all of the time? No.

Having a strong work ethic also means being accessible to your customers when they need you. While very pregnant with my second son, Derek—my due date only one week away—I still had many things to complete for my customers. I knew I would be telephone-accessible, so

I took the affirmative position and told my customers what I could do for them. I remember telling a prospective customer that I would be in touch within the week so that we could set up our next meeting. Looking at my condition, the customer couldn't help but ask, "Won't you be taking some time off?" I answered, "Absolutely, but I will of course be accessible by phone." He laughed at the thought of me having a phone in the delivery room. (Okay, so maybe I was unavailable for a few hours!)

Work ethic means finding ways to get the job done (in some cases several jobs!). This particular customer, as well as countless others, has provided me with numerous solicited and unsolicited referrals because he knows I will find a way to be there for him—when he needs me.

People who have a strong work ethic realize that even when they are faced with challenges, they do have choices. For example, I could have responded to my customer with "I'm pregnant: Please don't expect me to be available now for several weeks." No matter the circumstances, you always have a choice in how you will respond.

Average is unacceptable

Much of today's society seems to be looking for the easy way out. For example, I am amazed to find that more than 90 percent of the people who earn their living at sales have never taken the trouble to completely read one sales book! Most managers read only 10 percent of the management books they buy! You need to study to get your driver's license, but parents are not required to read a single parenting book, let alone attend a child development course. Many take the easy way out and just don't bother to learn to improve. We seem to tell ourselves we are okay just the way we are. In some areas we are okay, but in many others we are not.

How many years have we looked at our educational system and told ourselves, "It's not perfect, but it's one of the best in the world."? No more. Our educational system has gone from one of the greatest in the world to below average. According to E.D. Hirsch, Jr., in his book *What Your First Grader Needs to Know*, among 17 countries in 1970, American elementary students ranked seventh in elementary achievement. We dropped to 15th by 1980—third from bottom. It seems most would rather accept the way things are than work hard to return to excellence.

I have been privileged to work with people who are business superstars or fast becoming superstars. These individuals do not accept being average. Their day is driven not by the time clock, but by Determination. Often they begin work before sunrise and work past midnight!

My dear friend Dottie Walters (the one who gave me the final push to write this book) is a classic example of a brilliantly successful person. Dottie is a self-made millionaire and a highly respected guru in the world of professional speaking. The first thing you notice about her is her Determination! If you get the pleasure of meeting her some day, ask her how many hours a day she works. Her answer will undoubtedly be: "All of them!"

"I do not believe in a fate that falls on men however they act; but I do believe in a fate that falls on them unless they act."
—G. K. Chesterton, British author

The brawn-plus-brains approach

"Use your brains, not your brawn." Sounds good. But too many people use that as an excuse to sit back and carefully plan what to do next, then plan some more. Then plan some more carefully. You get the idea.

Brains without the brawn is nothing. By *brawn* I mean activity and accomplishment from that brain power. I have friends who are physically challenged who get more done in a day than others do in a week. When in doubt, action is better than sitting still.

Wake up and work at it!

Some dream of success; others wake up and work at it! A top salesperson may look like he or she can just sit back and wait for the phone to ring from those great old established clients. Success can appear effortless. Don't be fooled. What you don't see are the hours this professional has spent in strategies such as networking, prospecting and providing outstanding service to clients. No successful professional ever allows himself or herself the luxury of floating for very long—or else even the most devoted client will seek out other waters.

"If it were easy, everyone would do it" is a motto I live by. It wouldn't surprise you that apparently so do dolphins! In the wild, dolphins dive to depths of more than 1,000 feet and swim incredible distances. Stories about multimillionaires who sail around the world on their yachts as their portfolios continue to grow are seductive—and mostly false. In reality, the vast majority of successful men and women work 12-hour days to sustain and increase what they've built.

So, if while you are working you begin to think, "This is *hard!*" Yes! You are beginning to strengthen your work ethic. An increased work ethic will increase your success. The dream is not enough, you must wake up and work at it. Use your brawn—your activity—to accomplish your dream.

Practice and preparation make perfect

At sea parks, when people observe the ease with which dolphins achieve their magnificent high dives, they often get the false impression that such precision and elegance are instinctive, requiring little or no effort or practice. Not so! In between their training sessions, dolphins are left to themselves for free time. During night checks or first thing in the morning, trainers have often observed the dolphins practicing and rehearsing the new behavior they had just been introduced to. Why? Dolphins seem to be filled with Determination. From firsthand observation, I believe they take pride in their hard work and the amazing results it produces.

"By nature men are nearly alike; by practice, they get to be wide apart."
—Confucius

In all endeavors, precision requires hard work. Only after countless hours of effort do any of us develop a style and accuracy that can be reproduced on demand. A beautiful high dive only *appears* effortless—in any industry!

It is better to be doing a job, using your brawn, than sitting back and thinking, "What should I do next?" Often your forward action will stimulate your brain into thinking of ideas that far excel the ones you get while simply treading water or *floating*.

Please don't misunderstand. Dolphins don't seem to go out of their way to create extra work just for the sake of doing so—and neither should you. It's just that most great things can't be accomplished without a lot of hard work, practice and effort. As the old adage goes:

> *"If you always do*
> *what you've always done,*
> *you'll always get*
> *what you've always got."*

How to practice

When people watch me sell or coach an employee, they can't believe how I actually *do* all of the things I teach and how it appears so easy. That appearance is the result of years of practicing in front of mirrors, memorization and role-playing. At first when I began using these strategies, I felt silly, but I quickly realized how profitable the time I invested was. I now think of them as putting money in the bank. Top lawyers, actors, public speakers, politicians, businesspeople and salespeople all practice—and so should you!

If your business involves sales, practicing can help you and your team enforce important skills such as expressions, body language and choice of words. It helps everyone focus on the moment of delivery, to understand and feel how critical that moment is. Try practicing your sales presentation, an employee pep talk or your phone greeting in front of a mirror and audiotape yourself. Devote a minimum of 10 percent of your professional week to practicing. After you stop laughing and get back to business you will be able to critique your facial expressions, body language, tone and overall presentation. Another way to accomplish this would be to videotape yourself.

Managers: Practice motivating, coaching and communicating with your employees in front of a mirror, with peers or during a training session. When your team is together, use role-playing as a regular part of your meetings to prepare the staff for live encounters.

Preparation

Having told you to get going and exercise that brawn, I need to restate— the best strategy is a brains-plus-brawn approach. When your brain just isn't coming up with great ideas of what to do to help you reach your goals, your brawn can jump-start the process. Your brawn will get your brain going! However, you will not make a dynamic connection with people if you don't take the time to prepare and practice.

A dolphin by the name of Theresa was preparing for the birth of her new calf. Theresa's first calf had died because it ate a massive amount of mangrove pods. Prior to the birth of her next calf, Theresa spent much of her time clearing mangrove pods out of her section of the lagoon. She was able to use a brains-plus-brawn approach by learning from her unfortunate experience, taking the time to prepare properly for her next calf.

To be a dynamic success in business, you should use your Determination to examine and learn after each of your professional business encounters. This will help you prepare and practice for the next connection. The one time you are embarrassed because you didn't have a business card when asked should be all it takes for you to ensure that that experience will never happen again.

"Failure to prepare is preparing to fail."
—John Wooden, UCLA basketball coach

If busy hands are happy hands, then busy fins...

Josephine is a 30-something-year-old bottlenose dolphin who previously worked with the United States Navy. Josephine is a beautiful, large and powerful dolphin, who has been through quite a bit. She has deep scars from a shark attack. After years of outstanding service with the Navy, she was about to be retired to civilian life. The Navy personnel working with her felt that Josephine deserved to be retired to the Dolphin Research Center. They pooled their money and received clearance to send her there. Their only request was that she be free-fed (meaning that she would not have to work for her food). DRC graciously agreed, although soon after her arrival the team at DRC noticed that Josephine seemed to feel left out.

One day, without any training, Josephine completed a perfect routine with one of the dolphins next to her. She didn't need to do it for fish (she received that without performing behaviors). She obviously wanted to perform. Much like humans, Josephine seemed to want to excel and feel the sense of accomplishment and recognition for her labor, and was prepared to work hard.

If you want to be successful, you must perform a higher quality and quantity of work—faster—getting the most out of each day. These powerful and proven techniques will allow you to do just that.

Get the most out of your day

Most people know enough to be on time, so show others they are important by arriving 5 to 10 minutes early for appointments and meetings.

Here are other rewards of using your time wisely:
- Increased productivity.
- Increased profits.
- Impressing your customers with determination and organization, therefore creating an edge over your competition.
- Increased job satisfaction. If you are able to accomplish those things that are important to you, your job will be more fulfilling.
- Improved interpersonal relations. Because you have more time to spend on relationships, you feel more content, which will help make you more productive and profitable.
- More time to spend on work, play and family.

The Dolphin Dynamic

During many of my time management courses, I have uncovered numerous sharks that steal time. They include:

- Procrastination.
- Cluttered work surfaces.
- Looking for lost items.
- Interruptions.
- Lack of planning.
- Lack of prioritizing.
- Poor delegation skills.
- Wasted wait times.
- Worrying.

Some time-saving traits that highly successful professionals have mastered include:

- Having short-term and long-term goals.
- Using a planner, calendar or other written system to record priorities and activities.
- Working by importance rather than urgency, thereby avoiding procrastination.
- Prioritizing and then completing higher prioritized tasks first.
- Having clean and uncluttered work surfaces.
- Effectively dealing with interruptions.
- Delegating effectively and often.
- Using wait times effectively.
- Scheduling and committing to quiet time.
- Enjoying leisure time.

"Those who make the worst use of their time are the first to complain of its brevity."
—Jean de Bruyére, seventeenth-century
French writer and moralist

The importance of a carry-along planning system

Using a planner, calendar or other written system to record priorities and activities is critical to your success. Whatever system you decide on must allow you to plan, prioritize and record your daily activities. The system that I carry with me everywhere has impressed countless customers and saved me enormous amounts of grief by reminding me of scheduled tasks. It has made me a great deal of money by forcing me to face the sometimes unpleasant activities needed to excel, such as cold calls.

Some guidelines for using a planner:

- You need to be able to carry it with you.
- Make sure it has a phone directory so that you have no excuse for not returning calls. Phone entries for dynamic businesspeople will change frequently. Invest in the type with easily refillable and replaceable pages.
- Have a month-at-a-glance in addition to your daily pages. This will allow you to stay on top of your overall activity for the month.
- Make sure each day's page allows you to list and prioritize each task.
- Work by importance rather than urgency. The level of importance should be gauged by your short-term goals and your long-term Vision.

You'll read more about planning strategies and discover proven, highly effective techniques in Dynamic Three: Vision.

Procrastination sharks!

"I can do this later." "This can wait until tomorrow." Right. Then something else comes along and you postpone what you are working on until "later." First comes relief, then guilt, then regrets, then agonizing. This negative process probably takes more time than if you had actually performed the task in the first place, not to mention the positive feelings of accomplishment you gain by getting the job done!

Here is how to avoid procrastination:

- Write down everything you want to accomplish, no matter how insignificant it may seem.
- Prioritize your to-do list.
- Do your highest prioritized items first. These are often the most uncomfortable and difficult ones. Accomplishing these tasks will help you excel more quickly.
- If it is not possible to perform a task now, determine when you will soonest be able to perform it.
- Schedule it (write it in your planner—again).
- Keep your commitment!

If you need to work with procrastinators, remind them of deadlines in writing and use positive reinforcement when they complete projects on time or early.

Remove the clutter from your life!

A pile of paperwork is often a pile of postponed decisions (read my notes in the previous section, Procrastination sharks!). Cluttered work surfaces such as desks, tables, floors or any flat surface take away from your inner focus and peace and promote negative feelings. Here are some tips to keep you focused:

- Completely clear your desk before leaving for the day.
- Allow yourself 20 minutes at the end of each day for wrap-up. Take time out to write down notes that are fresh in your mind. The time it takes for you to clean your desk at the end of the day will be shorter than in the morning. Remember, your incentive at the end of the day is going home.
- File and learn to rely on your filing system. Many people hate filing because their filing cabinet is jammed full.
- Don't forget to move old files to a storage place on a regular basis. Add new space as needed.

Deal effectively with interruptions

"I really need your help! Please?" Sound familiar? Learning how to say no does not make you a shark. Dolphins are focused and don't let anything distract them from their course. While instructing my time management seminars, I am challenged by the many people who have such a hard time dealing with or avoiding interruptions. Most often the people who have the most interruptions and the most amount of work dumped on them (work that has nothing to do with them) are the people who are not good at saying no.

I know the thought of saying no is frightening to some of you. There are times when it is not a good idea to say no, such as when your boss asks you to do something or when a customer is involved. There are many times, however, that it is reasonable and essential to say no if you want to get your own work done. I am referring to the times that people ask you to drop everything and do their work. Even then, you should not be nasty when you say it. Quite the contrary. My favorite response is, "I'd be happy to help you with this; the first time I have available to assist you (looking in your planner, flipping pages and looking concerned) is a week from Thursday at 3:30...." What is most likely to happen is that the individual will go find a different dumping ground or will find a way to do his or her work without your help.

Dolphins handle interruptions in a variety of ways. Once Delphi was preparing to do a high dive. Normally dolphins communicate with each other well and move with each other in such harmony that it often seems magical. Well, Delphi eyed his target, prepared his strategy and zoom! He began his run to gain his momentum for the high dive when a newcomer to the area got in his path. Suddenly observers heard a big thud and white water was splashing high. Angry dolphin noises could be heard over the entire facility! Delphi was telling this newcomer, in rather harsh dolphin language, exactly how he felt about interruptions! After a long few moments, the fight was over, the newcomer slunk away with his tail between...well, you get the point.

Delphi's method was effective, but I don't recommend it in business circles. I think you would do better to try a few of my other strategies. The point is you are the only one in control of your destiny—don't give up the helm.

"The hours of folly are measured by the clock, but of wisdom no clock can measure."

—William Blake, English poet

Schedule and commit to quiet time

Dolphins know better than humans how important quiet time is. They don't appear to sleep like humans. Because dolphins are voluntary breathers, they must think about breathing, and hence, cannot afford to go into a deep sleep—they would drown. Besides, even if they could breathe while sleeping they would be vulnerable to predators. So, instead, they rest. When dolphins rest, they continue to swim. Theorists speculate that they shut down half their brain, which allows them to continue swimming, breathing and interpreting the sounds around them. They often swim more slowly, eliminating or minimizing their own clicks.

For humans, quiet time means a special time when no one will bother you. Often these golden moments seem impossible to find. Arrive at work 45 minutes before anyone gets to your office. You will accomplish a great deal more during this time. If you have an enclosed or separate office, close your door. This will minimize interruptions and give you prime time to accomplish your priorities.

Delegate often

"Nobody can do this work as well as I can!" "If someone else does this better than I do, I'm in trouble!" "I haven't got time to teach someone else to do it." "I want to be seen as a nice guy, not a dictator."

Sound familiar? These are big time-eating sharks in your life. Delegate! I recommend the following:

- Ask for help—don't demand it.
- Make sure the person has a clear picture of the purpose of any delegated work and knows what kind of results you expect. Take the time up front to lay out what you expect and when.

- Encourage questions.
- Let the individual you've delegated figure out the minor details.
- If the project is not going the way you would hope, ask if you can help out *this* time. When the project has been successfully completed, give lots of praise.

Use wait times effectively

Wait times are those times you are standing in line, sitting in your car, visiting the dentist, waiting on the phone, or any time you are waiting before you move ahead to the task at hand.

Car wait time. Use commute time productively. This concept has served me well. Much of this book was written on the New York State Thruway. While driving I wrote brief scribbles down on a pad that was propped up on the arm rest next to me. No, I didn't look at the pad. Later the notes were transcribed. Also, car phones are a great way to use wait time.

In-line wait time. These are great times to finish reading those magazines and trade journals you keep putting off. Keep at least one in your car with you, and when you suspect you may need to wait in line, bring it along!

Phone wait time. My friend Dottie Walters keeps several pads of paper on her desk. She likes to use the 8½" x 11" version with yellow lined paper. She heads up each one with the name of an article, speech or product she is planning. She explains in her book *101 Simple Things to Grow Your Business and Yourself*:

> *"Ideas will come to you as you wait on the phone or are speaking to someone. Jot them down. Don't lose them. Many computers now have 'note pad' systems that are quickly accessible from any program you are working in. These are just as effective if you are on your computer all day. If you must go over to your computer, turn it on, and launch the correct program—you may get interrupted or lose the idea before you can write it down. Keep one pad by your bed. Often a great idea will come to you in the middle of the night. Grab it! Write it down."*

On the topic of breaks, I don't recommend rest breaks. When you get tired, try substituting one activity for another, a change of pace such as physical to mental or vice versa. In my situation, when I'm working at the computer for an extended period of time, instead of "vegging out," I get up and straighten my desk, grab supplies or file.

Other techniques for using time wisely

- Avoid phone tag. Leave a message on your voice mail to update your callers on your location and schedule.
- Encourage callers to leave a detailed message so that you may call them back with a response.
- Conference calls are an under-used time saver. A conference call can reduce "go-between" phone calls, which cost time and can cause misunderstandings. When using conference calls make sure to let the people involved know in advance so they will be prepared.
- E-mail is fast becoming the way to communicate. Lilly Walters and I live on opposite ends of the country. For editing purposes, we sent this book back and forth almost entirely via e-mail. E-mail is inexpensive, much faster than mail (e-mail users call regular mail "snail mail") and more reliable.
- Use your date book to record all of the items you will be requiring the next day. It will help you avoid looking for lost items, plus you will not be rushed and you'll make fewer mistakes.

Leisure time

As hard as I work, it's often challenging to let go of work even for a short time. Realizing this, I also mentally prepare for pleasurable activities such as having a quiet dinner with friends, a day with my children goofing off or simply enjoying a few hours of solitude.

To successfully switch from work mode to leisure mindset, you need to decide what your objective is. For example, when I take time off to be with my children, have dinner with friends or have a few hours to myself, I simply remind myself that this is time off and my objective is to enjoy it.

Many people who work at a determined pace, give friends and family the "leftover" time. If this is the case, you will probably feel guilty and others will sense they're getting leftovers. People know quality time. This applies to your children, colleagues, friends, relatives and spouses.

Schedule time to work—and to play. When you look at play as important an objective as work, you will feel better about yourself and not feel guilty about spending quality time with family and friends. If you haven't accomplished everything you planned—reschedule, dismiss or re-allocate. This will give you a better sense of control.

Turn objections and obstacles into competitive advantages

The lights go out, the phone breaks, the car won't start. You can sit and wait, or you can look at the obstacles to your carefully scheduled life as advantages. Once again, use your brawn to climb over those obstacles!

When my friend Dottie Walters needed to bring in more money to help support her family, she didn't have a car and she didn't have anyone to watch her children. She had choices. She chose to begin a tiny advertising business on foot. She would call on potential clients pushing her two babies in a broken-down baby stroller. By the way, she lived in a rural community with no sidewalks. She didn't see these situations as obstacles but as a constant reminder of her motivation to succeed! She built that business into four offices, 285 employees and 4,000 continuous contract advertising accounts.

I once found myself challenged, as a salesperson at a waterbed store, by a woman who had returned with her husband to look at a complete bedroom set. She walked in with her husband and her little boy. Instantly her 3-year-old was terrorizing the showroom: tearing off bedspreads, knocking over display items and whining. What I wanted to do was ask the parents to tie him up (only kidding...sort of). I knew that if I didn't somehow involve this "cute little tyke" in the sales process he was going to get the best of me and I was going to lose my sale.

I wish I could have videotaped this transaction. I was juggling keeping the darling occupied so that Mom and Dad could make a positive decision without interruption, and at the same time keeping an eye and ear on them. I was listening and watching for positive or negative conversation and body language so I knew how and when to respond. I heard positive conversation and saw positive gestures so I brought my little friend over to Mom and Dad and closed the sale. But this was not the end. I commented on how much their child liked the beds and, yes, they also purchased a new bedroom set for their son.

After that learning experience, I immediately went out and bought a coloring book and a box of crayons to make the next situation easier. Now I recommend giving the child coloring sheets that have your product and store name on them. That way if the parents don't buy today, you can have the child take the coloring sheet home to hang on the refrigerator! Your Determination will help you find ways to use your brain plus your brawn in looking at obstacles as advantages.

Overcoming objections

How do you react when someone raises an objection or turns you down flat? Salespeople realize that objections are part of their business, but in reality objections are part of all business. Other examples of objections—in a nonsales environment—are: someone, a boss or colleague, not responding to one of your ideas positively; not receiving a raise you were anticipating or felt you deserved; or being questioned about a procedure.

Whatever you do when confronted with such an objection, do *not* become defensive. You can appear slightly surprised and respond with a positive response, taking into account their comments. If you appear defensive or dejected when you're met with objections, you might kill the communication, leaving the waters open to your competitors.

The next time you come up against such circumstances, think about the way dolphins approach challenging situations. For the most part, these animals take control and find solutions to virtually any obstacle placed in front of them. They face, avoid and conquer sharks and other obstacles along the way. So can you, if you stay open and positive.

View objections as tests of your Determination. I've learned that dolphins have unique ways of testing humans. Once while I was sitting on the docks at the Dolphin Research Center, a dolphin named AJ brought me a leaf. I took it from him and we began to play catch. After three rounds back and forth, AJ opened his mouth and dropped the leaf onto the back of his tongue. He kept his mouth, which was filled with some 88 razor-sharp teeth, wide open. I reached in, took the leaf and resumed our game.

A dolphin trainer saw this interaction and later asked if I was concerned about reaching into the mouth of a dolphin. "No, should I be?" I asked. "Probably not," she answered. "AJ seemed to be testing you. Apparently you passed his test."

The trainer went on to explain that, in the past, AJ had tried this game with others. When a human was too frightened to take the leaf from his mouth, the dolphin left, as if in disgust.

The parallel is striking. Customers constantly test people in business. In this interaction, AJ was testing me. The fear some people have of putting their hand inside a dolphin's mouth is no less terrifying than the fear of failure or rejection a businessperson may experience when a customer raises an objection.

Turn objections around

Recently I was coaching a salesperson, attending a real, in-home sales call with him. The customer greeted us at the door and curtly explained that his neighbor had purchased our product and it wasn't working. At that point, the salesperson had a choice. He could have taken this objection as an opportunity to show the customer how concerned he was about customer satisfaction by asking for the neighbor's name and phone number, and by promising to follow up and rectify the situation. Or, the salesman could have argued with the customer, saying that there must be something wrong with this unsatisfied neighbor.

Unfortunately, this particular salesman chose the second alternative. First he asked if the customer was sure that her neighbor hadn't bought a similar product from a competitor. A serious mistake. The customer may not have even known about the competition. Why would he want to reveal this information? Also, it is generally not a good idea to disparage a competitor's product. As the old adage goes, "Whenever you throw mud, some stays on your hands."

Fortunately, the customer was momentarily distracted and had to leave the room for a minute. I took full advantage of the opportunity to whisper a little message in that salesperson's ear: "Don't ever argue with the customer...no matter what!"

Ultimately, when the customer returned, we were miraculously able to turn the situation around. But, generally, mistakes like this end up blowing the sale.

Determination to be a dynamic communicator will help your brain to think and your brawn to act. Determination will help you uncover your customer's real needs. Feeling dejected and rejected are almost reflex reactions, and it's easy to give in. Turning an apparent negative into a positive takes a lot more work, but the results are well worth the effort.

It's easy to become anxious or defensive when confronted with an objection. But be warned: If you take an objection as a personal attack, the customer will sense your defensiveness and any interest will quickly dissipate. Your mission will not be accomplished.

Turning a negative into a positive takes practice, discipline and a certain amount of guts. I can guarantee, however, that the results will speak for themselves. Consider the advantages of viewing objections as opportunities rather than attacks:

- Salespeople will enjoy stronger closing ratios and higher average sales.
- Managers will improve rapport with employees, superiors and customers.
- Customer-service people will build stronger relationships with customers who suddenly seem less difficult.

I know how hard it is to maintain openness when an objection is hurled your way. This is especially true if you believe in your product or service and feel the criticism is unjustified. Still, I would urge you to follow these tips:

- Do not become defensive. Instead, look curious and slightly surprised when someone gives you an objection.

- Respond with "That's a good question," and then use the *feel, felt, found* technique: "I understand how you feel, others have initially felt that way, but what they have found is, after purchasing (or whatever you want them to do), is (something very positive that they will care a great deal about)."

- I have excellent success with the "recall strategy" as well. I use things that they have said to show the importance of what I am trying to convince them of. They can't argue with their own words very well, but they can argue with yours— you are the salesperson.

   For example, let's say you are selling fine jewelry and after an excellent presentation of your product, your customer responds by saying, "It's lovely but it's so expensive." Use the recall strategy by courteously and respectfully responding, "Jim, earlier you said that quality was something that was important to you. Is this the type of quality you were referring to?"

"We can convince others by our own arguments, but we can only persuade them by their own."
—Joseph Joubert, French moralist

Follow-up systems to foster success

Most of the people you will be competing with won't exhibit a high level of Determination. In sales, a lack of Determination can be deadly to success. Therefore, a high level of Determination will give you a competitive edge. For example, when a customer leaves without buying, don't give up, follow up!

Recently I did a training session on follow-up approaches. Within 40 minutes after the first training session, a salesperson reported closing a $600 sale, which he directly attributed to this follow-up system!

The goal of a sales presentation should be to close the sale while with the prospective customer. However, what about all of the customers who didn't buy that day? It's a costly mistake to ignore them!

Many—way too many—salespeople will sit and wait for the next customer. This is a mistake. Don't give up—follow up! If you are filled with Determination, you will quite naturally think of ways to follow up with the customer who just walked out the door. Look around for new ways to find what that customer wants, and call him or her back, drop him or her a postcard, a thank-you note, e-mail, fax, whatever! Follow up. Now you have the chance to make a dynamic impression and a powerful connection with this last customer, and the one you are hoping will come in the door next.

A study done in high-end retail sales showed that the customer who didn't buy the first day was most likely to buy within 24 to 48 hours after his or her visit. Different industries and products will vary slightly (72 hours or under is a good average). Imagine you have a less-than-72-hour window of opportunity.

A step-by-step follow-up system

In order to follow up with your customers, you need their full name, complete address and phone number, and a system to gather this information. A survey card is one system that I have found to be extremely successful. The survey card can be used when a customer is leaving without buying—or after a sale—as a means of following up, requesting referrals and notifying the customer of future sales.

A preprinted, two-part carbonless form on card stock with no more than five questions works best. I recommend the title to be "ABC Marketing Survey" or "ABC Advertising Survey." Here is an example of a survey card for a furniture store:

ABC Marketing Survey

How did you hear about ABC Company?
TV ___ Print ___ Radio ___ Other ___

What products were you interested in?_____

_____

Are you aware of our free, in-home decorating service?
Yes ___ No ___

What suggestions do you have for us? _____

_____

Name:_____
Address:_____

_____
Phone number:_____

Thank you for the opportunity to serve you.

This survey card will provide valuable information, including the customer's name, address and phone number for customer follow-up. Ideally, the salesperson would have already found out the customer's name during the sales process.

The way this card is presented will determine the response. If the salesperson simply asks the customer to fill out the card without an explanation, approximately 50 percent of the time the customer will not complete the card. To increase the number of completed cards, salespeople should explain to their customers that they are doing a marketing/advertising survey to determine their company's effectiveness and they would like their help. Then they should hand the customer a pen and ask him or her to fill out the card, explaining that it will only take a minute or two.

Most customers have some indication that advertising is expensive and they will think of your company as astute if you monitor it. Also, many customers will feel important when asked their opinion. Following this method, the customer will almost always agree to fill out the card.

Stand with them while *they* fill out the card. This is the step that en-sures that they will fill it out completely. Thank them when they are done and begin a conversation regarding the products they were in-terested in. Do not be surprised if your customer decides to buy from you today, even though he or she previously said they needed to think about it. This is in part because you have a name, address and phone number. He or she may think, "What if he calls me back?" Most people don't want to be embarrassed by telling you they bought some-where else.

If the customer does leave without buying, I recommend following up within 24 hours. Within this window of opportunity you can call the prospective customer and drop him or her a personalized, handwritten note in the mail. We will discuss handwritten thank-you notes in de-tail, including actual examples in Dynamic Four: Enthusiasm.

The telephone is the most effective form of follow-up. Here is how the untrained person makes a follow-up phone call:

"Hi, Mr. Johnson, this is Mark from ABC Jewelry. When you were in yesterday, you said you needed some time to think about the watch you were looking at. I'm just calling to see if you have decided yet."

No, no, no! Don't lead with your chin! A better strategy would be to introduce yourself and your company, remind the customer of all of the great benefits they most liked about the product or service—and give him or her one or two additional reasons that you may not have covered during your initial meeting.

"Hi, Mr. Johnson, this is Mark from ABC Jewelry. Remember the watch you were looking at—the one with the 14 karat gold band? Well, I wanted to make sure you knew that it does come with the manufacturer's five-year warranty and you have your choice of either bronze or off-white face. Which face would you prefer on your new watch?"

(Always assume the sale, knowing your customer is going to buy it— you're just asking which color.)

Managers, role-play these follow-up situations with your salespeople. Remind them that like any other new situation, it will be uncomfortable at first but the investment they make in time and energy will be well worth it.

If you don't obtain the sale on the first phone call, how often should you call? Until you get the sale. Determination often prevails when all else fails.

Postcards or notes alone are a second follow-up approach. The message on the postcard or note should be exciting, personalized and brief. However, this approach is not as effective as a phone call because it is a one-way communication and it doesn't encourage as much excitement.

Whichever method you choose, you are building a stronger relationship with your customer, illustrating to your customer you are interested in earning his or her business and probably showing up your competition. Also, you will double the effectiveness and profitability of your investment in advertising.

Determined image: what customers see

One of the many reasons we feel drawn toward dolphins is their dazzling appearance. They aren't like most mammals. They don't have fur. They have a friendly, sleek, yet powerful and dynamic image. It is also their attitude—the image from the inside and outside that draws us to them.

One excellent way to enhance your attitude is to fix up the outside first. You've heard the expression, "Fake it 'til you make it!" It means that if you pretend you are, let's say, "Enthusiastic," before too long you *are* Enthusiastic! The same with image. If you dress yourself to look successful and do things that make you look like a person with Determination, Instinct, Vision and Enthusiasm, you will soon actually become that person!

In this section, we will work on ways to enhance your personal image and the image of your company.

One way I show my customers I have a strong work ethic is by not sitting down in a reception area. When waiting to see a prospective customer, I look over company materials to obtain any information that will help me in my customized qualification and presentation. But the main reason I don't sit down is because when my prospective customer greets me, he or she should meet me eye to eye. If I'm sitting, he or she will tower over me and I will not have the ability to make a dynamic connection. This little difference begins to set me apart.

I also don't carry a purse. In my opinion, carrying a purse is making a statement that I'm female. I don't want my prospective customers to think of me in terms of gender. I want them to think of me as a person who cares more than enough, is extremely capable of solving their product and/or service wants and desires, and who has a great work ethic. There is absolutely no reason women can't carry everything they need—wallet, makeup, etc.—in a briefcase.

It may seem superficial to some, but the importance of creating a dynamic image can never be underestimated. There are exceptions to every rule, but most top professionals put a great deal of effort into developing the right image.

Look at highly successful people in any field. In most cases, they have an exceptional image—one that reflects a can-do attitude and makes them stand out from the crowd and the competition. Improving your image will have a direct impact on improving your financial status. You don't have to look like a movie star to project a great image. All you have to do is make the most of what you've got. But it takes work.

- It's easier to present an image that is merely ordinary, acceptable or sloppy. That involves less risk and less money.

- It's easier to have materials that are not well-thought-out or elegantly presented. That takes less energy and less money.

- It's easier to throw on an unpressed suit, unpolished shoes and walk around with your hair a little messed. That takes less time.

The dedicated and disciplined professional realizes that a little extra care and preparation time is well worth the effort, even though the initial payback may sometimes be hard to measure.

If you are in business, and if you are a normal human being, by the end of the day you are not going to be fit for human companionship if you don't take personal hygiene very seriously. It is very difficult to make a connection with anyone if you're unappealing to be around.

Be conscious of your body's visual appearance and hygiene. Whether you are a man or woman, your hair and complexion should be neat, clean and fresh. Your face should be pleasant to look at. For women, your makeup should be sophisticated (up-to-date but not trendy), light (not caked on) and appealing.

I recommend carrying a complete travel case in your car, a toothbrush and lots of mints in your briefcase. Freshen up every two hours. These are keys to always having a fresh and dynamic appearance.

Smoking, gum and food

Recently, I was assisting a company interview to fill a sales position. We accepted phone inquiries and resumes, and then set up personal interviews. We were particularly looking forward to meeting with one of the gentlemen we had spoken with. He was outgoing and had great credentials. As my clients and I were preparing for the interviews, we noticed an individual sitting in his car, lighting up a cigarette. When we realized that this individual was the applicant we were so looking forward to meeting, the owner of the company got up and refused to meet with him. The owner's reasoning was that if this person would do this for an interview, he would certainly do that for a meeting with a client. I agree.

In another instance, I was conducting a sales training seminar for a group of new salespeople. I deliberately waited until after their first break to discuss my opinions on smoking. They were surprised and concerned that I recommended that they do not smoke before, during or after a sales appointment. They understood not smoking during a sales appointment but were confused why not before or after. I explained: not before, because you can smell the smoke on them and that might offend the customer. And as far as the *after* part, when you get in your car and light up right away, you look frazzled, unprofessional and needy. Not the type of image you want to project.

In addition, if you are on your way to another sales call, that *next* customer will be able to smell the smoke on you. My last point was that most people were not thoughtful where they extinguished their cigarettes when they were around nonsmokers. My point was made when I asked the smokers in the group where they had put out their cigarettes moments earlier. They sheepishly admitted: on the grass of our office complex.

If you haven't given up smoking yet, do it—*now*! Not just for your health (though that should be a good enough reason in itself), but because you are blocking all those people who *don't* smoke from making a connection with you! Even if you don't smoke around others, we all know you smoke. We can smell you coming from a distance. You are sending a message to the person with you that you are a nervous person, dependent upon an unhealthy and unwise habit.

Gum has a similar effect on others. Please understand that I would love to chew gum. However, I don't want to chew gum so badly that I would risk my professional success for it, so I don't chew gum! People around you become either fascinated or annoyed by your jaw moving and the obnoxious sounds that follow. They won't truly hear your message.

As a leader or future leader in the companies I have worked in, I have always tried to avoid situations that tend to project an image that is "too comfortable." For example, I generally don't eat with others in the workplace. Yes, I eat (I bet you guessed that!). But when I do it's generally in my office with my door closed, reading an industry magazine.

I generally don't eat with my employees, co-workers and, of course, never in front of a customer—unless it is at a meeting where we are enjoying a meal together. Now there are exceptions such as a slice of celebratory cake or a department pizza. But generally I find it better to focus on work rather than food.

Clothes that create a dynamic image

Your clothes should give you a crisp, clean, professional image. "Professional" has many interpretations and depends on the industry you are in. Look at what the executives in your industry are wearing, and go a step beyond. If you are selling hay and feed to farmers, "professional" would mean something different from selling software systems to NASA. But maybe not too different.

While consulting for the construction equipment industry, I suggested that our salespeople dress up more than they had been before I began with the organization. Boy, they didn't like the idea of buying new clothes. They complained that it wasn't practical to be walking and crawling around construction sites and vehicles in a tie and pressed long-sleeved shirt. I explained that it was logical to me. It was going to increase sales. I went on to tell them how impressed their customers would be when they did show up in a shirt, tie, coordinated belt, polished shoes and dress slacks. After a month, without hearing a word from them, I finally decided to ask if they felt the improved image had served them well. They agreed and, yes, their sales were higher.

If you are selling to an industry that is trendy, like the hair products or fashion industry, you can be more flamboyant, but always stay on the conservative side. When someone comes to you it will be for "business"—and the business side of business is never "trendy."

Whatever the standard is, make it sharp and clean. Watch the next time UPS makes a delivery. Their crisp, clean, reliable image is one reason UPS continues to be successful in a very competitive industry.

Gentlemen: In business-to-business sales, a white shirt has been proven to help develop credibility and trust. Ties are generally a must. Additionally, ties in red or navy help promote a dynamic image. The suit should be well-tailored and fashionable, not too trendy. Darker-colored suits tend to generate credibility. Coordinate and match your belt and shoes.

Ladies: Even if the fashionable skirt length is very short, stick with a more conservative length. In business-to-business sales or a professional office setting, blouses tend to make a more professional image than sweaters. I know—this is disappointing to me, too. I love sweaters but I reserve them for off-work time.

I have a few strategies that work for me in my industry. As I mentioned, I don't carry a purse—I carry a briefcase. Also, I prefer not to wear suits that are stereotypical of women. Unlike women's suits, you would never see a man's suit without lapels. So, I prefer to wear suits with lapels. I do not try to appear masculine; I just don't want to make an overpowering statement of femininity.

Whatever the choice of clothes that you wear, it is critical that you pay special attention to the care and presentation of your clothes. See that all your clothes are spotless, pressed or ironed well, and your shoes polished. I buy the $2 shoeshine kit in the supermarket that gives my shoes a polish in a second. Great investment.

How important is your image? Let's say you sell copiers and the average copier sale is $4,000. Will your image assist you in gaining or losing a $4,000 copier sale? Yes! If there is any incongruity between the quality of your product and the quality of your image, you are planting seeds of doubt in your customer's mind. If your clothes are wrinkled the customer may think that you don't care about yourself and therefore you may not care about the product you are selling or your customers.

I realize that dress-down days are becoming a more popular alternative in the business world. Dress-down days originated in the 1980s as a no-cost vehicle to improve morale among white-collar workers stunned by salary freezes, layoffs and increased workloads. Dressing down is supposed to mean a relaxed professional look.

Unfortunately, many companies that have tried this concept have done so without drawing very clear pictures for their employees. This relaxed policy often results in employees who arrive for work looking like they just rolled out of bed.

Overall, I feel that dress-down days have some merit but have numerous drawbacks. Let me address this from a few angles. If I were a businessperson looking to become very successful, I would not participate in dress-down days. It is critical that you be perceived as a successful professional.

As a business owner or manager, I would consider dress-down days on a very limited basis. In Buffalo, for example, Wegmans, a very progressive grocery retailer, has dress-down days that coincide with community events such as Buffalo Bills football games. Generally, however, you can find their employees in white shirts, black bow ties, black pants, clean smocks and engraved name tags. Occasionally they wear company casual shirts that promote their slogan—"Wegmans, where every day you get our very best!"

As an employer, take the time necessary to specify your expectations for dress-down days because you do not want to have to discipline your employees for something that was designed to be motivational.

Remember, most customers probably could buy the same or a similar product for less. Why, then, is this prospective customer going to buy from you? An attractive, polished, successful appearance encourages your customer to have confidence in you—and in your product or service. That confidence will give you the edge over competition.

Where to find help on what to wear

Do not use fashion magazines as a source of what to wear in business. Most fashions seen there are *never* seen in a real business setting.

Instead, keep your eyes open when you are reading business magazines and your own industry publications. When you see pictures that you like, clip them out and review them before you buy an outfit. Think about the mood you want to create with your image. Which of those pictures makes you feel that mood? Well, that is the image you want to emulate.

Ask yourself these questions:

• When I am the boss, what will I dress like?

• Do I like the way I look now?

• If money were no object, what would I do to change my image?

Once you answer these questions, you will know what will make you feel like you have a dynamic image. Chances are, if you feel that way on the inside, you look that way on the outside.

I have given this advice to many salespeople who've responded, "I don't have the money." My response is, you don't have a choice when it comes to creating a dynamic image. Beg and borrow if you have to. Do whatever you need to do to get good-quality clothes today, not tomorrow. When you buy them, buy fewer, better-quality items rather than more, lower-quality items.

Manners

Let's jump back to what your attitude looks like from the inside-out. Beauty may only be skin deep, but *rude* goes clear to the soul. A plain and average-looking person can be the most popular, merely because he or she is kind and uses good manners. Nothing will enhance your image as well as these three things:

- Say "please."
- Say "thank you."
- Present a sincere smile.

Using these three simple principles often will help you connect with people around you much better. These simple steps will give you and your company an edge over the competition. In the Enthusiasm Dynamic, I will refer to the work of Letitia Baldrige, author of *Executive Manners*, to discuss other manners and how they will help you make a dynamic connection with your customers.

"Good manners have much to do with the emotions. To make them ring true, one must feel them, not merely exhibit them."

—Amy Vanderbilt, U.S. author
and etiquette expert

Image: business environment and tools of your trade

In addition to your clothes and manners, consider all aspects of the image of your company. Everything associated with your company will reflect a Determined attitude (or lack thereof).

Studies have found that a highly organized and attractive work environment increases employee productivity. Studies have also revealed that your customers will feel more secure and comfortable in a clean environment. In other words, a messy or even moderately organized work environment is costing you and your company money. (Dolphins also seem to enjoy a clean environment. While working with them, I have found that they'll bring me scraps of plastic and debris, as if to say, "Would you get this garbage out of here?")

The cleaning of a work environment should be done *after* the close of business for two reasons: The employees performing the work have motivation to get the work done quickly and the employees walking in the next day with be entering a pleasant, clean and organized work environment. There may be minor exceptions to this, such as picking up trash from a parking lot or sweeping the front walk.

Be careful, however: Many employees take it upon themselves to start cleaning, vacuuming, etc., during the last 30 minutes before customers have left. Bad move. That will make customers entering during this time period feel rushed and unwelcome, as if they are intruding. Make it clear to your team that cleanup is done after all customers have left. Will it cost a little more for that 15 minutes of cleanup time? Yes. But your customers will appreciate and reward the extra effort.

Reception areas and parking lots

When you walk into your place of business, take a good look at what your customers see. It is very easy to overlook the dirt in our own homes—we somehow just get comfortable with it. That little nick in the wall or the grease spot in the corner—we just start to ignore those things. But your customers are coming in with fresh eyes. They will see them.

Your reception areas and your parking lot are reflections of the quality they perceive they will receive from you. Make sure those first impressions are a reflection of your company's Determined can-do attitude to provide excellence. Design a systematic way to check on a regular basis that the company's image is spotless.

The tools of your trade

As important as your clothes and grooming are to helping you enhance your attitude and image, your materials are also important. Take a close look at your company letterhead and business cards as well as other presentation materials such as corporate brochures, media kits and similar printed pieces. Consider other "tools" of your trade, such as your briefcase or pen. All should reflect a successful and polished professional image.

When a prospective customer or co-worker sees materials with rough edges, he or she makes negative subconscious assumptions. These assumptions could include a belief that your handling of paperwork is sloppy, that you have poor follow-through skills. Any material you carry should be clean and in like-new condition.

By the way, what does the inside and outside of your car look like? Is it clean and neat? I worked for a gentleman who felt that a car was an important thing to talk about during an interview process. He would ask applicants if they had reliable transportation. When they answered in the affirmative, the owner would ask what kind of car they drove. After they told him, he would say something like, "That's a great car, what color did you choose?" He would excuse himself to make a phone call. He was actually headed to the applicant's car! He wasn't concerned about the newness of the car but he was concerned about the cleanliness. He believed that how you kept your car was a reflection on your paperwork and overall follow-up with customers.

Team shirts

The same image advice applies to owners when they are trying to make a dynamic impression and set themselves apart from the competition. Team shirts or uniforms are a great way to make a dynamic impression, appear more credible and set yourself apart from the competition.

In retail that requires a sales associate to stock and carry merchandise—such as in the home-improvement industry—high-quality polo shirts with the company logo embossed on them work great. Chase-Pitkin, a progressive home-improvement company in western New York, did a customer survey (we will talk about why and how to do this later). It learned that one thing customers wanted was more help. Customers wanted to be able to find an employee when they needed assistance. This company put all of its employees in bright yellow, high-quality polo shirts.

Within a short time, many customers commented that this particular store had more employees than at other locations. Not true. It had the same amount; it just appeared that there were more employees because they were easily identified by their bright yellow attire. As a bonus, this also served as a security plus by making employees more visible to potential shoplifters.

Companies that require their salespeople or employees to be more professionally dressed may consider using team shirts for installers or delivery people. Do not discount the role that these people play in delivering your product or service. Often they are the last people your customer sees.

Team shirts are an investment and an excellent way to make a splash in today's shark-infested business waters. (Employees should sign an agreement that indicates their responsibility for caring for and returning the shirts upon termination of employment.)

Using name tags is another excellent way to add credibility and help your customers feel like they are dealing with an individual rather than just a nameless employee. Invest in name tags that are engraved rather than the punched-out version. The latter give the impression of temporariness.

Checklist for a dynamic business image

Image is a very personal issue. The following are proven strategies that work. Next time I come to your company and work with your people, we can discuss any areas you may disagree with. Until then, please try these:

Image tips from the outside

- Look stylish—not trendy.
- When people look at you, your clothes should not overpower you.
- All of your clothes should be clean and pressed.
- Your attire should be right for the weather.

- Hands should be clean and properly manicured.
- Shoes should be polished (they also need to be resoled and reheeled often).
- Shoes should be the same color or darker than your outfit.
- Your clothes should be comfortable.
- Double-breasted jackets should always be buttoned.
- If you remove your jacket for comfort while you are alone, it is a mark of politeness and respect to put your jacket back on when greeting someone of importance (any customer).
- You should be well-groomed at all times (hair, teeth, nails).
- Take a break every two hours and freshen up.
- Make sure your jewelry is not overstated. (One or two rings, one necklace, if any. Gold personifies success more so than silver.)
- Extend your excellent image into your materials and your business environment.

Women

- Never wear a sheer blouse.
- Wear an appropriately collared blouse, preferably one with a raised neck line.
- Make sure suits are well-tailored and professional.
- Make sure your hemline is an appropriate length.
- Always wear nylons with a skirt or dress.
- Don't carry a purse.
- Sweaters are generally not a good clothing choice in a professional setting.
- Eliminate use of perfume, or make sure it's very subtle.
- Apply makeup with a light hand.
- Don't wear overpowering jewelry—necklaces or bracelets that jangle, earrings that dangle or rings that encumber a handshake.

Men

- Always wear dress socks in a business setting.

- Never wear short socks—wear them to the knee or at least calf length. When you sit down, your customer or client should never see a bare leg.

- In a professional setting, *always* wear a tie.

- Always appear clean-shaven. Mustaches are acceptable if well-trimmed. Beards should be avoided.

- Wear dark, well-tailored suits.

- Wear white, gray or light-blue shirts.

Other tips

- Use great professional manners—always find ways of saying please and thank you.

- You're never fully dressed without a smile!

- Allow your demeanor to show tremendous work ethic.

- Don't sit down in a reception area.

- Make sure all your "tools"—binders, business cards, pens— have a dynamic appeal.

- Always have your business cards available—and always request one in return.

Part of the dolphin's appeal is its supreme confidence. As playful as dolphins are, they appear extremely confident in their abilities. Extremely successful professionals also have a confident attitude, which makes them more attractive to potential customers. This attitude of Determined self-confidence shines from the inside out.

Salespeople always sell more when they are confident—first, because they *believe* they will sell more and, second, because customers find a confident attitude compelling and reassuring. Successful managers and leaders of all types also have an attitude of Determined self-confidence. Self-confidence is essential for creating a can-do attitude.

> *"Confidence contributes more to conversation than wit."*
> —François, Duc de La Rochefoucauld,
> French writer and moralist

Determination is a can-do attitude

Determination can be inspired by many things: fear, hunger, hurt, love, hope. Something inside tends to kick in when you really need it or want it. How can you initiate Determination? By telling yourself, "Yes, I can do this," in all types of situations. One example of a can-do attitude in action is the 80-year-old woman lifting a car off her grandchild who was pinned under it.

> *"Immense power is acquired by assuring yourself in your secret reveries that you were born to control affairs."*
> —Andrew Carnegie, U.S. industrialist
> and philanthropist

I had a similar experience one day when my sons and I were down by our pond playing by the water. Suddenly I heard a piercing scream from my older son Craig. He was covered with wasps! He had stepped on a nest and was frantically trying to swat them off. I darted toward him, swooped him up in my arms and ran a quarter-mile up a hill to our house. Hours later when I was sure Craig was all right (he was sure he was all right after a few minutes, I was traumatized for hours—this mom stuff is exhausting), I realized that I had run with my 50-pound son in my arms up that hill's steep incline. I normally can't walk up that hill without pausing to rest.

If you are Determined enough, your body and spirit will find a way to help you get the job done. As that 80-year-old woman had, I too had manifested a can-do attitude. We both recognized a need to act and we told ourselves, "Yes, I can do this," and we did.

Just like Natua who was not willing to accept the defeat of the humans that day in Dolphin Therapy—he simply was Determined and kept looking for one more way to get the job done. One more way— that is all you need to look for when you find you are confronted by an obstacle.

Determination is a resolve, a commitment to saying and believing, "Yes, I can do this," and not stopping until the job is done! Determination prevails when all else fails. Find what it takes to reach inside yourself.

Believe in yourself

"If you believe you can, or you can't, you are right."
—Henry Ford

When I was about 15, Dad and I were talking about my future. There was a woman running for the town mayor. Dad said he was glad she was running, but he was a bit disappointed. He thought I would be the first woman mayor. "That's okay," he said. "You can be the first woman president if you want to." At that time I didn't know I only had a few months left with Dad. I know there are millions of people out there who were not as lucky as me. Millions who've never had someone who believed in them as much as Dad believed in me.

It is wonderful to have someone there telling you, "I believe in you!" But when they are not there, you must believe in yourself. Many of the greatest successes I have had came about mostly because I was Determined to show the disbelievers they were wrong! A can-do attitude must begin from the inside.

"I get it done, not because I believe I can get it done, but because I know I can get it done—this is not the same."
—Dr. Edson Bueno, founder and president of a billion-dollar series of companies in North and South America

Associate with "great-attitude people"

Whether you are a salesperson, customer service rep, manager or business owner, there is a direct correlation between manifesting a positive attitude and obtaining top income and performance. Positive attitudes are contagious, and by hanging around others who share your attitude you will be enhancing your own.

Bad attitudes are just as contagious. Be careful of people with bad attitudes because they have the ability to bring you down. You wouldn't let a person just reach into your wallet and take a handful of money from you, would you? Of course not. But that's exactly what your complaining co-workers are doing every time they say, "We're just priced too high," or "Nobody's buying this time of the year," or "The economy is bad," or "Our manager/owner just doesn't understand." Avoid these people like the plague. Don't let them pull you under, or get in your way. When they try to bring you down, change the subject, find others to talk to or go do some follow-up calls.

Attitude is everything.
—Zig Ziglar, author and motivational speaker

By associating with good-attitude people, you are helping yourself create a can-do attitude. Keeping people with great attitudes on your team, whether they work for your company or are part of a network of vendors who help you get your job done, will ultimately enhance your attitude and help make you more successful. People who have great attitudes and are able to keep that same attitude even during difficult times are rare finds in today's business waters.

Once in a great while someone really takes my breath away by making incredible strides to please customers. I have the pleasure of having Kinko's Copies as one of my company's vendors. They help me and help my clients by providing exceptional quality and service. My company does a great deal of duplicating of workbooks and handouts so I work with Steve Reilly, the general manager of a Buffalo, New York, branch quite a bit.

During a seminar in Buffalo, at 2:40 p.m., I suddenly discovered that my client had unexpectedly invited an extra 20 people to that afternoon session! Although I had allowed for more than enough workbooks, that number still put us a few short. I took a shot at Kinko's. Fortunately, Steve answered the phone.

"Steve! Does your branch offer delivery service?" I asked, desperately. "Laura," he replied, "we do now. How can I help?" What a great can-do attitude! "The delivery is only part of my challenge," I warned. "I need 10 booklets copied, collated, bound and delivered all by 4 p.m." That left less than two hours.

"Steve, it is very important that they be delivered on time for a prompt start." Within 15 minutes, Kinko's driver was there to pick up my originals. At 3:45 p.m. I was paged to the reception area of my client's business. Who was waiting for me, package in hand? Steve himself!

He could have simply told me, "What, are you nuts?" I'm sure he was at least thinking that. He could have simply "hoped" he would be able to accomplish this project, and complacently waited for his delivery person to make it back to me on time or not. But he did neither. He took matters into his own hands. Steve's attitude of Determined self-confidence not only shines from the inside out and the outside in, it spills over to his entire company. Steve and Kinko's continue to exceed my expectations.

The mind-body connection

Dealing with responsibility is a requirement of success. Since responsibility and stress tend to go hand in hand, dealing effectively with changes and/or stressors is a requirement to becoming more successful. Countless studies show us a healthy body enhances a positive, can-do attitude, increasing productivity.

Exercise. By exercising regularly, I experience lower stress levels, clearer mental processes, confidence in decision-making and better mental vision. In addition, I feel better and look better—more fit, toned and self-confident.

Specifically, I have chosen jogging as my ongoing daily regimen of aerobic exercise. The reason I jog instead of going to the gym or walking is that it's quick and convenient, providing all of the wonderful benefits of a good workout. The benefits of aerobic exercise in reducing cardiovascular disease, the number-one killer in the U.S. today, are well-documented.

The biggest complaint I hear when it comes to exercise is that people say they don't have time. If you want to get ahead quickly, you don't have time *not* to exercise! Commit to 40 minutes five days a week.

The return on the time investment is enormous—physically, mentally and financially.

Nutrition. Putting in long hours and a quick-paced day can be draining on your body's supply of energy. Whether you are on the road all day or sitting from nine to five, fast food has a way of creeping in as a daily staple. Most fast-food restaurants now have nutrition brochures. Ask for them at the fast-food places you frequent most often. Try that hamburger *without* the cheese and mayonnaise. You get rid of about 15 grams of fat. Better yet, have chicken or a salad with low-fat dressing.

I am a firm believer in supplementing with vitamins. The benefits I have noticed are enormous: virtually no colds or flu, a better complexion and lower stress. When I interviewed doctors, I chose a physician who felt that vitamins play a role in good health. Find someone who is knowledgeable and willing to answer your questions and discuss the numerous considerations in choosing vitamin supplements. In addition to vitamin supplements, force yourself to eat fresh vegetables and fresh fruit daily.

Sleep. Trust me, I know how your day's work can intrude on your sleep time. I know how the next day must begin on time. I have heard and read about programming yourself to exist on less sleep. I tried it. The result, however, was a sluggish Laura with cranky, subdued tendencies. I make a conscious effort to get at least eight hours of sleep per night. Much of the time I come very close. When I don't, I do my best to catch up.

Don't wait for a great day—create one!

While selling retail at one of my first real sales positions I became acquainted with Larry. He was in his late 60s, kindhearted, hardworking—the perfect grandfather/Santa Claus type. He had an extraordinary ability to relate to his customers. At times he would be the jolly fellow that people enjoyed being around. With younger couples he was the grandfather type who gave good, sound advice. At all times he was an intriguing person whom everyone trusted and enjoyed doing business with.

Larry consistently ranked among the top three salespeople. He never lost his ability to work with customers and friends, nor his top rating as a salesperson. This, despite being diagnosed with cancer and actively dealing with it. Although he must have been in pain often, his Determination, Instinct, Vision and Enthusiasm made him one of the most lovable and successful people I have ever known. I don't know why he kept going like the Energizer bunny, but he did. He seemed to radiate an attitude of joyful self-confidence. He didn't wait for a great day—he created one with what he had to work with.

You can't wait for everything to start going well to have a great can-do attitude. Things will start to go well when you turn your attitude around.

"We cannot adjust the winds, but we can adjust the sails."

—Unknown

Rejection and resilience

People with can-do attitudes do not let rejection discourage them. Instead, they are resilient and look for better ways to get the job done. The best baseball players fail to hit the ball every time. In fact, the players with the greatest records for hits also have the greatest records for misses! They just tried more often and harder. No one will succeed every time.

Even if you are practicing the Dolphin Dynamics brilliantly, you will not be perfect and you will be rejected. It is part of the process of success. The person lying in the corner with a towel over his or her head rarely feels much of anything—neither the thrill of victory nor the agony of defeat.

Rejection should not be taken personally. When a prospective buyer says no, or you are faced with difficult customers, they are more often rejecting the product or service you are offering, not you. Be resilient. Try again. Trying is much better than staying on the ground. Use your can-do attitude and look for another way to get the job done.

> *"Vitality shows in not only the ability to persist but the ability to start over."*
> —F. Scott Fitzgerald, U.S. author

Learn!

In the 1870s a bishop who had charge of a small denominational college made his annual visit and stayed with the school's president. The bishop boasted a firm belief that everything that could be invented had been invented. The college president thought otherwise. "In 50 years," he said, "men will learn how to fly like birds." The bishop, shocked, replied, "Flight is reserved for angels and you have been guilty of blasphemy."

The name of the bishop was Milton Wright, who had two small sons— Orville and Wilbur.

The world is changing every day, and you are changing with it. The only way to keep up and stay ahead of the competition is to learn. Learning is also a brilliant tool that not only keeps you competitive, but helps to keep your mind resilient. "If you always do what you've always done..." (Oh, I've mentioned this already?) Then what do you need to do differently to change your attitude? Learn!

Build a library in your home. Use inexpensive bricks and boards, stack them in a corner, whatever, but create a library! Don't forget to read the books you put there!

Learn! Plan on three hours a week to learn something new. In addition to the intrinsic benefits of learning, a knowledgeable person is just more interesting to be around!

How can you learn?

- Read! I don't mean just fiction. I am very frustrated when I do a sales seminar and learn that greater than 90 percent of the sales and customer service people I come in contact with have not completed one business book. This is frightening.

- Listen to tapes! I don't mean the Beach Boys! Stock up on motivational and educational tapes—listen to them while you're getting in that morning run—or find yourself stuck in traffic.
- Watch TV! I don't mean "Lucy" reruns. Turn to The Discovery Channel, as well as educational shows.
- Engage in formal study. Check your local college for a list of credit and noncredit classes available to you.
- Take personal-development courses and read personal-development books.

Balancing home and work ethic

When I need to travel, I miss my family the second I step on a plane. One way I console myself is by the knowledge that children will not learn a strong work ethic if they don't see their parents displaying one. My Determination to succeed includes a strong desire that my family will feel my love and caring even when I travel—which, because I'm a trainer and speaker, happens rather often.

People with a strong work ethic work hard at all aspects of life, including family. Balancing home and work commitments can be achieved. If your business life pulls you away from your family, try some creative ways to make dynamic connections with your family. I use these:

- Before I leave for even one day, I take out the markers and leave a colorful note and picture for each of my children and my husband, Joe. Usually this prompts a return card or note, which makes my return wonderful.
- I always try to phone them each morning and evening to keep abreast of their day-to-day activities.
- Little notes and cards in the mail to each of my children makes them feel special.
- From the road I draw a simple cartoon of my day or of all of us together doing something fun and I fax it to each of my sons. I ask my children to color it for me so I can see it when I come home.

- I always make sure my family has a fax number so they can send me notes and pictures.
- Once, I noticed cute smiley-face cookies at an airport bakery (the kind my sons loved). I shipped them overnight back home with a note, "Thinking of you makes me smile, here are a few smiles back!" Yes, I sent one to my husband, too.
- I send balloons. If you have time and want to save the money, blow them up yourself before you leave. Once, before my youngest son Derek was born, I decorated the kitchen with an "I Love Craig" theme. He loved it!
- Sometimes I make Joe his favorite dessert, and leave it for him in the fridge.
- I hunt at gift shops for small souvenirs of my trips and drop them in the mail.

Using Determination to make a dynamic connection with your family will help ensure personal and professional success. Don't overlook this important part of your life.

It's lonely at the top, but what a view!

Determination will occasionally be viewed by your peers as unfavorable. If you work hard and achieve success, some will envy you. It is one of the costs of success.

The more you advance in hierarchy, power and professional achievement, the more you will encounter sharks in your business waters—and many of those sharks can even be co-workers, associates and competitors who are threatened by your success.

Yet, as you strengthen your work ethic and drive, new people, more dynamic and successful, will be attracted to the new you. The view from the top will be breathtaking, even if you are a bit lonely at first.

"Never give in except to convictions of honor and good sense."
—Winston Churchill

Quiz for the Determined Dynamic

1. Are you accessible to your customers whenever they need you?
   ❑ Yes   ❑ No

2. Do you read the business or management books that you buy?
   ❑ Yes   ❑ No

3. Do you act on your ideas rather than just plan out your moves?
   ❑ Yes   ❑ No

4. Do you devote time each week to practicing and developing your skills?
   ❑ Yes   ❑ No

5. Do you effectively use wait times?
   ❑ Yes   ❑ No

6. Do you prioritize your work by importance instead of by urgency?
   ❑ Yes   ❑ No

7. Do you stick to your priorities?
   ❑ Yes   ❑ No

8. Is your desk cleared at the end of each day?
   ❑ Yes   ❑ No

9. When necessary, are you able to say no to others when asked to drop everything to help them?
   ❑ Yes   ❑ No

10. Do you schedule and commit to quiet time?
    ❑ Yes   ❑ No

11. Do you avoid becoming defensive when faced with objections?
    ❑ Yes   ❑ No

12. Do you regularly follow up with customers—even those who don't buy right away?
    ❑ Yes   ❑ No

13. Are you making a conscious effort to improve your professional and physical image?
    ❑ Yes   ❑ No

14. Do you make it a point to say "please" and "thank you"?
    ❑ Yes   ❑ No

15. Are you able to keep a positive attitude in the face of adversity?
    ❑ Yes   ❑ No

16. Do you take care of your body—exercise, a healthy diet and sleep?
    ❑ Yes   ❑ No

17. Are you determined to have a great day, every day?
    ❑ Yes   ❑ No

18. Do you constantly look for more ways to get the job done?
    ❑ Yes   ❑ No

19. Do you keep your home and work lives balanced?
    ❑ Yes   ❑ No

20. Do you believe in yourself?
    ❑ Yes   ❑ No

If you answered 18 to 20 yes's, you exhibit a high degree of dolphin-like Determination and will increase your success rapidly.

If you answered 13 to 17 yes's, beware—sharks are in the water with you.

If you answered 10 to 12 yes's, you are wounded and sharks are moving in.

If you answered nine or less yes's, *get out of the water*—you are about to be eaten alive!

Checklist for the Determined Dynamic

- Do not accept being average! Aim higher.
- Look for one more way to get the job done when the last way didn't work out.
- Remember, you *always* have choices.
- When in doubt, action is better than sitting still.
- Work at your dreams!
- Don't wait for your brains to kick in; using your brawn first will often help your brain get working to assist you.
- You will do better to DIVE in and make mistakes, than not to act at all.
- Remember, if it were easy everyone would do it.
- Busy hands are happy hands. Humans enjoy the sense of accomplishment and recognition of their labor.
- Perfection takes practice and preparation.
- Practice your communication skills in front of a mirror.
- Don't just be on time, be early!
- Plan time for your family and your leisure.
- Work by importance rather than urgency.
- Prioritize and then complete higher-prioritized tasks first.
- Have reading material and tapes available for unexpected wait times.
- Use a planner.
- Brighter days start with a cleaner desk.
- Learn how to politely say no when necessary.
- Schedule and commit to quiet time.
- Objections are part of business, so turn them into positives.
- Be ready to make new friends who share your level of drive.
- Don't give up, follow up (and develop a system to do it)!
- If you always do what you've always done, you'll always get what you've always got. Plan on doing something different.
- Part of the dolphin's appeal is its supreme confidence. Find ways to enhance your own confidence.
- Associate with positive people. Avoid negative people!

- Believe in yourself, even if others may doubt you.
- Plan at least three hours of exercise a week.
- Eat healthy! Avoid fast foods, get plenty of fresh fruits and vegetables and add vitamin supplements if necessary.
- Do the best you can with what you have at your disposal right now.
- Build a library in your home.
- Learn! Plan on three hours a week to learn something new.
- Take a serious look in the mirror. What would it take for you to look like the dynamic person you dream to be? Take steps today to look like that person!
- Take a look at the materials you hand out. Are they immediately perceived as professional and dynamic, conveying the image you want to convey?
- Take a look at your business environment. Do your customers see what you want them to see?
- Do you smoke? Give it up!
- Say please and thank you—often!
- Say to yourself daily, "Yes, I can and will do this!"
- Make yourself available to your customers at all times.
- Take pride in your hard work, and the results it produces.
- Don't procrastinate. Keep your commitments.
- Allow 20 minutes at the end of each day for wrap-up.
- Learn to rely on your filing system.
- Ask for help when you need it, and make sure the person helping you understands the task.
- Keep paper handy, and use it as ideas come to you.
- Look at obstacles as tests instead of as roadblocks.
- Keep your workplace clean—but do it after business hours.
- Find ways to make your image more visible (team shirts, logo, name tags, etc.).
- Don't wait for a great day—*make* one.
- Don't take rejection personally. Try again.

In conclusion about Determination

The techniques described in "Dynamic One: Determination" offer ways to develop a strong work ethic, accomplishing more in each day. Increasing and displaying a strong work ethic will help you connect to customers, clients, associates, co-workers and bosses by separating yourself from the many sharks. This dynamic will help others trust and respect you.

There are three kinds of people: People who make things happen, people who watch things happen, and people who wonder what happened. Be the first type of person—do something to make the connections in your life stronger and longer lasting.

It takes 21 days of consistent practice to become comfortable with new techniques or ideas. I mean 21 days of consistent behavior. So practice the attitudes, behaviors and actions that you want to become a permanent part of your life.

Don't wait for your ship to come in...DIVE in! Swim out to it—with Determination!

Dynamic Two: Instinct

In this dynamic you will learn:

- How unleashing your professional sonar will increase sales!
- Top performers are excellent explorers.
- Questions to master and questions to avoid.
- How to identify Determined, Instinctive, Visionary and Enthusiastic internal and external customers.
- How to establish rapport, even with difficult individuals.
- How, when and why to discipline and motivate employees.

Instinct: an innate capability or aptitude

One of the dolphin's most intriguing and powerful traits is its ability to interpret and understand subtle signals. This skill in humans has been called a sixth sense, an intuitive perception, supposedly independent of the five senses. We all have it. Most people don't use it. Top performers, however, do!

If you deal with people and you want to be more successful, you need to develop this skill. We all have the ability to read these messages. However, most people have not taken the time to develop the power to read, interpret, understand and connect with those around them.

Reading silent signals

A boy who suffered a stroke that paralyzed his foot and leg underwent conventional physical therapy to encourage movement. Unfortunately, this young boy wasn't cooperating by doing his exercises. His mother, who lived near the Florida Keys, decided to try a "dolphin swim." Without being cued by the trainer, a dolphin circled the boy, went underwater and began tickling his injured foot with its mouth. The next thing they knew, the little boy began kicking.

How did the dolphin know what was wrong with this boy? How did he know which leg was afflicted, or that movement would be beneficial for the boy?

One theory is that dolphins use *echolocation,* a highly developed form of sonar, to detect injury in the human body. They have even detected new pregnancies in human females who didn't realize they were pregnant.

When using echolocation, dolphins emit clicks and whistles that project a high or low frequency sound. These sonic signals are reflected by objects in their path. The returning echo is received and interpreted by the dolphin. The sonic image enables the dolphin to discern size, density, speed, direction and other characteristics of objects— even minute objects in murky waters.

In addition, dolphins appear to be very sensitive to subtle, nonverbal messages from humans. If a dolphin is not focusing, cooperating or behaving properly during a training session, trainers may turn their backs on it. This is similar to a "time out," given to misbehaving children by parents or caregivers. Just like children, dolphins seem to crave socialization and human interaction. They seem to view a time out as "no fun," and, therefore, avoid repeating the behavior that earns them the time out.

Just as scientists believe that humans use only a small amount of their potential brain power, we appear to tap into only a tiny fraction of our Instinctive sonar. We all have the ability to effectively interpret people's movements. In a business or professional situation, such "sonar" can help us determine others' moods, feelings, insecurities, readiness to move forward and more. Unleashing our Instincts will help us tune in to the individuals we encounter, encouraging them to become more emotionally involved, creating a win-win situation for everyone involved.

Tools to better understand people

Without being told, dolphins adjust their pace to match a fragile, challenged child, and then will frolic enthusiastically when someone like me jumps in the water with them.

You do the same thing. Imagine yourself talking to a newborn baby. Imagine you are talking to another adult during a football game. Imagine you are talking to an elderly and dignified woman. Imagine you are talking to a friend in the grocery store. I am confident that you alter your own communication style to better relate to the person in each situation.

Dynamic connections are made by using the same ability to shift your style to match the person you are communicating with in every situation, especially those situations where their differences are less obvious.

To determine these differences, I use:

- Observation of body language.
- Personality style analysis.
- Career profile assessments.
- Handwriting analysis.
- Observation of environment.

Observing body language

People who are not disciplined in using and interpreting body language may find it easier to neglect this critical nonverbal form of communication or pretend that it doesn't exist. Most people are not willing to invest the time or energy to master this pure and powerful form of communication. I compliment those of you who are willing to make the investment. The payoff will be astounding.

Reading body language is not as mysterious an art as you might think. It requires more logic and common sense than anything else—because nonverbal communication is simply a physical response to what we're thinking. For example, when you hear a shrieking noise, what do you do? You cover your ears. That's body language! And when a child sees a frightening movie? He closes his eyes or covers his head. More body language.

Sometimes it's a little more subtle. The employee receiving a negative review from her boss may not cover her ears if she doesn't like what she's hearing. But she may lean toward the door, communicating her desire to remove herself from the criticism.

What about some other examples? Such as when you're talking about something you're not sure of—perhaps you have to explain a missed deadline or goal? You will probably mumble, closing your lips and making the message harder to hear. You may cover your mouth with your hand—another muffler. Without consciously realizing it, your mind sends a message to the hand, "Hey, I'm about to say something I'm not sure of, try to stop it." (When a customer mumbles or covers his or her mouth, I watch carefully for other signs of insecurity or evasiveness.)

While playing basketball, I was taught to watch my opponent's knees while guarding. Players usually turn their knees in the direction they are planning to move. I've found this to be true in business, too. If, for example, a customer is facing you, directed toward you, you're doing great. You have captivated his or her interest. If, all of a sudden, your customer turns away from you and crosses his or her arms, you'd better think about what you just said that caused this "close-down." When a salesperson is in the midst of a situation such as this (which happens much more frequently than most people realize), he or she should rewind, consider clarifying what was just said, and readjust the pace or the content of the presentation.

While in furniture sales, I was presenting a bedroom set to a couple. Everything was moving along great and then the husband closed up, crossed his arms and began walking away. I immediately rewound the tape in my mind and realized all I had said was that the bedroom set was solid cherry. Well, I quickly and nonchalantly asked the husband how he liked the solid cherry bedroom set. He turned back toward me and asked me to show him the construction. I happily did so. He told me he once bought a dining room set and the salesperson had told him it was solid wood—but it wasn't. He was pleased to see that I was not only truthful, but was able and happy to demonstrate the benefits of my product to him.

If I hadn't carefully watched his body language and quickly followed up with an open-ended question, in all probability the customer would have wandered around the store, politely thanked me for my time and left. Instead, I used the tremendous tool of body language interpretation to identify that something was going wrong. This allowed me to substantiate my statements and continue to build the customer's trust. The end result was a very loyal customer who now very much enjoys his solid cherry bedroom set.

Using silent signals to understand others

When we rub our necks, it often means we are tense and frustrated. As we tense up, the first nerves and muscles to react are the ones closest to the top of our spinal cord. Our bodies realize that these muscles are tense and tell our hands to rub the neck to relax the muscles. All of this happens without conscious thought.

The more you use your natural sonar skills, the more your ability to read people will grow. Until that time, it helps to know what some of the silent signals may be telling you. The chart on pages 74 to 76 shows negative and positive signs to look for.

Working within protected territories

Humans, like many other species, carry around a type of bubble, and within it they remain in a guarded and protected safety zone. This bubble is relaxed in correlation to their comfort level to the people around them. This bubble has four zones. The closest—the intimate zone—is just under 18 inches. This zone is meant for only the most intimate of contacts, a significant other or close family members, for example. Then there is the personal zone, which is between 18 inches to 48 inches. Those allowed in this zone are individuals you are quite comfortable with, such as co-workers, friends or relatives. The social zone is from 4 to 7 feet. It is generally for people you are unfamiliar with but now have dealings—a vendor, perhaps, or a new boss. The farthest, most distant zone—the realm of strangers—is the public zone, which is 7 feet and beyond.

Silent Signals: Negative

Negative signs	Meaning	Effective response
Folded arms	Uncomfortable, anxious, defensive or cold	Review what you just said. Regardless, get them out of that position by getting them involved. Try handing them something.
Rubbing neck	Frustration or fatigue	Rewind the tape of what was said that made them feel uncomfortable or anxious. Try a compliment.
Avoiding eye contact	Disinterest, low self-esteem, preoccupation or possible dishonesty	Grab their attention by an excited voice, get them physically involved or try a compliment. Look for other signs of possible dishonesty.
Shaking head side to side	Disagreement, disbelief	Build positive agreement by verbally agreeing with them on something they have already said. Then you can subtly address their opinion.
Pointing finger	Generally an aggressive gesture	Smile, use pleasant, not challenging, eye contact. If you can, agree with them on something, subtly nod your head up and down.
Hands flat, palm down	Dominant position	Let them feel they are in control by nodding your head up and down and by using submissive gestures.
Frantic, nervous look on face	Insecure, nervous, uncertain	Offer verbal reassurance with positive messages, such as, "We are going to take care of this for you."
Hand supporting head	Boredom	Use enthusiastic gestures, vary your voice, smile and use eye contact.
Hands in pockets	Insecure	Be positive, reassuring and take the friendly lead by using open-hand gestures.
Eyebrows raised	Suspicious	Be excited and offer a compelling statistic, favorable to your position.

Negative signs	Meaning	Effective response
Turning body away	Boredom, suspicion or preoccupied	Grab their attention with an exciting gesture or involving question such as, "John, what do you think about this?"
Hand covering face or mouth	Uncertainty or possible deceit	In the likelihood that they're uncertain, offer information that may reassure them.
Rapid eye blinking	Nervousness	Check your body language to make sure you're using open-hand gestures and nodding, as well as reassuring statements.
Blowing cigarette smoke upward	Extreme confidence	Allow control. Use language such as, "Well, I'm sure you are aware that..." Nod your head up and down.
Blowing cigarette smoke downward	Possible deception	Look for other deceptive signals such as lack of eye contact, rapid eye blinking and covering of mouth.
Eyes shifting from side to side	Nervous or possible deception	Look for other deceptive signals such as covering of the mouth and lack of eye contact. Ask leading questions to determine the "truth."
Pushing away from a table or situation	Signals desire to get away or conclude discussion	If possible, conclude the discussion quickly, or work to regain interest— identify a benefit, lean toward them, even ask them if they're concerned about something you've said.
Timid handshake	Shyness, passivity	Use slightly smaller gestures and quieter tones.
Rubbing neck, looking away, crossing arms and turning body away	You're in serious trouble	Run! (Just kidding.) Something you've said or done has triggered a negative reaction. Figure out what it was—and change the behavior immediately.

Silent Signals: Positive

Positive signs	Meaning	Effective response
Eye contact	Interest, receptiveness	Smile back and enthusiastically move on.
Nodding head up and down	Agreement, attentive	Feel confident moving on to your next step.
Open palms	Honesty, possibly asking for assistance	Listen carefully to the words and use reassuring gestures and expressions.
Smiling	Positive attitude, openness	Feel confident moving on to your next step.
Relaxed arms and upper body	Open and receptive	Smile and move forward.
Rubbing hands together	Excitement, anticipation	Run with their excitement and get them involved by moving forward with your presentation.
Leaning forward	Interest	Continue with dynamic gestures and expressions.
Extended open hand for shake	Receptive	Smile, establish eye contact and shake hands.
Body faced toward you	Interested in you and/or your message	Smile, face them, establish eye contact and move forward.
Patting you on shoulder and back.	Interested in getting closer to you.	Smile and move forward.

These distances are, of course, preferences and not always realities. Clearly, when we ride a crowded bus or elevator, we sometimes allow strangers to trespass into our intimate zone. When we attend a meeting with new business associates, or go to a concert with casual friends, they may be sitting well within our personal zone. But when circumstances allow, these boundaries—invisible though they are— are quite real. If you're skeptical, try this: The next time you're in an uncrowded public place like a library, take a seat right next to another individual. That person will probably look at you with surprise, even worry. He or she will probably squirm and scoot the chair away from you—or even get up and move.

So which zone should we be in most of the time if we want to connect with our customers? Often, body language books will tell you the social zone (4 to 7 feet) is where most businesspeople stand when they conduct business. Not me. I am not the usual business person. I believe you make a statement with your distance or lack of it. Most businesspeople don't connect with their customers. But I do, and you can, too.

When you maintain 4 or more feet of distance from someone else, you are presenting yourself as a stranger. But if you are speaking with someone, you are *not* a stranger. To make a dynamic impression and a connection with someone, I recommend that you step in a little from your comfort point to just under the 4 feet mark. Many people need to overcome fear of rejection to stand this close.

If you observe someone pulling away, perhaps turning his or her body away, having trouble making eye contact and squirming, you may be making the individual uncomfortable. Simply take a small step back and see if he or she relaxes.

Step into the personal zone with an "I'm interested in getting to know you" smile and making friendly eye contact. By using these gestures, including a welcoming handshake, you will help establish a connection. You'll be perceived as a friendly dolphin rather than feared as a threatening shark.

Match their pace

Many people are leery of and threatened by a 40-pound dog. However, most people are not only comfortable with, but dazzled by, being in the water next to a 400-pound dolphin. While doing research at the DRC, we were informed about the tremendous power in the dolphin's tail. The tail is the dolphin's power source, which helps it travel at speeds up to 25 miles per hour. Before we were ever allowed in the water, we were informed to avoid the tail area in order to prevent injury.

Here I am in a dorsal pull between two magnificent and powerful dolphins, AJ and Santini.

Enthusiastic soul that I am, I got into the water and, of course, didn't think much about the "tail thing"...until I was between two dolphins, Santini and AJ, in the midst of a dorsal pull. As I was hanging on to their dorsal fins, I thought about the fact that I was between two 400-pound dolphins and, worse, my lower body was directly between their tails. Just then we crossed over a small wake of water and I unintentionally shifted left. My legs were underneath a dolphin!

In the split-second it took me to realize this, somehow not just one, but both, dolphins simultaneously shifted left with me. They never touched or hurt me. That split-second interaction was the most memorable. How did they know? Did they sense my fear? Did they feel my movement? How? Because they were not just plowing ahead, they took the time and energy to be focused on their "customer"—me. I hope they felt my relief, appreciation and amazement for their concern and talent. If two 400-pound dolphins can make me feel comfortable in their environment, salespeople and businesspeople can surely make customers feel comfortable in theirs and we must, if we want to survive in the competitive waters that surround us.

Dolphins do not take advantage of weaknesses of the humans they help. Instead, they make interactions exciting and pleasurable. Whether you are a salesperson, manager or dolphin, it is almost impossible to make proper adjustments without first realizing the differences of the person you are with. To use our sonar abilities we must discipline ourselves to intensify our observation and listening skills, so we will know just what to adjust and how. The tools I have given you so far, and those to follow, will help you match the pace of your customers, therefore assisting you in forming a strong connection with your customers and the people you work with.

How to adjust the pace

A dolphin's pace is fast—as yours should be. However, even the best presentation of your thoughts—whether you are a salesperson, business owner, manager or you are having a personal conversation—will be wasted if you are moving too fast for the individual you are talking with. Although I fully understand that communication is a two-way effort, it is the responsibility of the *sender* (the one with the message to send out), not the receiver (the one receiving the message), to adjust the pace of the conversation to the comfort level of the receiver.

How do dolphins determine the varied speeds of their dorsal pulls? They are incredibly Instinctive. We believe that dolphins do not fully understand the human's audible form of communication. They do, however, seem to have mastered the innate ability to watch and understand the most subtle nonverbal cues and adjust their actions.

Have you ever been in a conversation and someone used a word, phrase or reference with which you were unfamiliar? Did you stop the conversation and ask for clarification? The more uncomfortable you were in the situation, the higher the chances are that you didn't interrupt the conversation and ask for clarification.

Customers, for example, are generally uncomfortable when they enter uncharted waters—an unfamiliar place of business. They don't know whether to expect dolphins or sharks. Likewise, employees entering the boss's office for a review may be wary of the unexpected.

Whether you are a manager or a sales professional, you can pick up on this discomfort from nonverbal cues. The individual may move guardedly, slower than normal. He or she may avoid eye contact or seem to eye you suspiciously, searching for nonverbal cues from you. In a sit-down situation, the individual may choose the chair farthest from yours. He or she may appear to "hug" himself or herself in a protective gesture.

If you witness such body language, you'll know to match your pace to the individual's, avoiding plowing ahead with your agenda and further intimidating him or her. Don't move at a fast and furious pace, speaking quickly, or, no matter how strong your presentation, it will have been a wasted effort.

As you sense an increasing level of comfort in the individual, you can cautiously increase the pace, using your Instinct. If you're effective at this, he or she will acclimate to the situation and be open for a connection.

On the other hand, I've witnessed numerous situations where salespeople were boring their customers to tears and didn't know it. They had no awareness of their customers' "pace."

Remember, communication needs to be a two-way effort. Watch the movements and nonverbal signals of those you work with. I watch my customers like a—no, not a hawk—like a dolphin.

To verify that the pace of my sales activities is appropriate, I look for signs of frustration, confusion and boredom from my customers. When they appear bored, I grab their attention by handing them something, getting them moving or speeding up a little bit at a time, until I see any signs of agreement—nodding, smiling, eye contact and open body signals.

When a customer appears confused, I accept responsibility and apologize for not making myself clear. I say something like, "I'm sorry, I get so excited by this product and the great benefits it brings people, I sometimes cover this information too quickly. Let me take a moment and review the important aspects of this (product) and what they mean to you." This is in contrast to, "Oh, I see you didn't understand."

In an employee review situation, if you see signs of confusion, take responsibility: "I'm sorry, I'm going too fast, let me review and clarify my thoughts." Again, by assuming the responsibility for clear communication, you make the employee feel more secure and receptive.

Exploration: encouraging signals

As a dynamic, Instinctive communicator, you must be prepared to lead. Many people are just too shy, nervous and uncomfortable to ask questions. This may result from swimming in far too many shark-infested waters and being bitten. Our approach will give you many ways to effectively connect with people you will be dealing with.

Exploration is one of the most important stages of communication. It involves questioning, researching and understanding—verbally and nonverbally—before you offer your suggestions. You need to find ways to encourage others to communicate with you so you have enough information to work with in order to make a dynamic and correct presentation of products or thoughts.

Prescription without examination is malpractice

Let's say you went to a doctor with a pain on your right side. He or she—without asking about anything other than your insurance coverage—said you needed immediate surgery. How would you feel? I would feel a lot better if the doctor questioned and observed my symptoms and researched my condition, showing interest in me.

We all know that prescription without examination is malpractice. Unfortunately, many business professionals and salespeople do what this doctor did. Even before they are certain what the prospective customer is interested in and what will be best for them, they immediately ask, "How much do you want to spend?"

Fortunately, this kind of person does not last long in a successful business environment. I recommend that you avoid asking how much your customer wants to spend. In most situations, you are causing more trouble than it's worth because the customer will generally not know what your product or service *should* cost. (Do you know what an appendicitis operation costs?) If they do know how much it costs, they will tell you less than that number. Now you have to work backwards. There are many smart questions you can ask, and we will discuss them later in this section, but, "How much would you like to spend?" is not one of them.

Visual exploration

When entering someone's office, the dynamic Instinctive individual will discover a wealth of evidence—clues and information that will help paint a clearer portrait of the individual he or she wants to connect with.

I have one customer who decorates his office with pictures of dogs. I complimented a particular picture hanging on the wall. He proceeded to tell me about the breed and went on for a few moments about his interest in dogs. He is an avid dog lover and breeder. I told him I was a dog lover also! He asked what kind of dog I had—connection! Now the conversation was between Laura and Jim, not Laura the salesperson and Jim the guy with money.

In another situation, I noticed that a customer had numerous ducks in his office—pictures, figurines, etc. I used the ducks to break the ice, which led to more informal conversation. During this time, he revealed that he and his wife had just adopted a baby. After our meeting, I sent him a congratulatory note and a soft baby teether/rattle in the shape of a duck. He called me to tell me that it was his favorite toy (I was a bit worried the baby might never see it!).

The little present was a small investment. Since then, Greg and his company have purchased thousands of dollars of product from my company and I feel I have a new friend.

Visual exploration is a skill that both humans and dolphins use to create dynamic connections. I personally experienced the dolphin's skill at visual exploration at the Dolphin Research Center. At the conclusion of one of our workshops, the attendees were allowed to ask the dolphins to perform behaviors of our choice. My request was the "present" behavior, a stunt the dolphins first did on their own, without training. Subsequently, the trainers taught them to perform it on command.

Normally when dolphins bring presents, they bring seaweed, twigs, jellyfish or anything else they feel like. Delphi went down deep in the water, out of sight. He was gone quite a long time. So long, in fact, that the trainer with me was about to recall him. Just then, Delphi popped out of the water with the biggest piece of coral I have ever seen! It was so large that his mouth seemed to be straining to hold it. He could have brought me anything of any size or shape. Delphi sensed that this unusual piece of coral would please me. It certainly did! More important, Delphi was thrilled with himself—just as thrilled as I was when I found just the right gift for my "duck" friend.

When you walk into someone else's environment, take the time to observe. You will find positive ways of surprising and pleasing your customers. By doing so you are well on your way to building dynamic connections and making a more impressive splash in today's business waters.

Exploring personality styles

For centuries, humans have been trying to analyze people and categorize them by personality type. Even ancient Babylonians saw the natural divide of such types and developed one of the earliest personality studies. They divided all people into earth, wind, water and fire.

Most have found that people divide nicely into four distinct groups. As society and science have advanced, other studies have been conducted and other classifications developed—interestingly, four still seems to be the "magic number" for classifying personality types. A few of them follow:

Personality analysis classifications

Earth, Wind, Water and Fire. Hermes Trismegistus or Thoth, Astrology.

Thinker, Intuitor, Feeler, Sensor. Dr. Carl Jung, 1930. Jung developed the introvert concept.

Dominant, Inspirational, Steady, Compliant. *Performax* by Dr. John Geier, University of Minnesota.

Amiable, Analytical, Expressive, Driver. David W. Merril and Roger Reid, from *Personal Styles and Effective Performance.*

Extroversion-Introversion, Sensing-Intuition, Thinking-Feeling, Judging-Perceptive. Myers-Briggs.

Domineering, Submissive, Pleasant, Unpleasant. Albert Mehrabian.

Director, Relater, Socializer, Thinker. Jim Cathcart and Tony Alessandra, from the album "Relationship Strategies," (Nightingale-Conant, 1984).

Applying the concepts of personality analysis to the Dolphin Dynamics will enable you to determine how to make a dynamic connection with your customers. The diagram on the following page illustrates the four dynamics and their associated characteristics.

Each of the four categories represents aspects of an individual's personality. If an individual is a *Determined* personality, he or she is task-oriented, direct and fast-paced. An *Instinctive* personality is nonassertive, somewhat reserved and relationship-oriented. The

Visionary person is self-contained, task-oriented and nonassertive. And you'll find an *Enthusiastic* personality outgoing, quick-paced and relationship-oriented.

	Self-Contained—Task Oriented		
Non-Assertive, Indirect, Slower-Paced	*Visionary*	*Determined*	**Assertive, Direct, Fast-Paced**
	Instinctive	*Enthusiastic*	
	Open—Relationship Oriented		

Most people are not purely one personality or the other. Generally, we do tend to exhibit more characteristics of one type, while showing some traits of the other types. The goal of a professional in today's shark-infested business waters is twofold:

- To recognize his or her personality type and strengthen the traits he or she may be lacking.
- To recognize the personality types of others—co-workers, bosses, customers and clients—in order to better communicate with them.

If a person is very strong in only one classification, he or she will have a tough time connecting with others. For instance, the extreme of the Visionary would be Mr. Spock, from "Star Trek." The extreme of the Enthusiastic would be Muppet heroine Miss Piggy. A human who exhibits either extreme level of these personality types would not do well in today's business environment. Understanding where your own weaknesses are will help you target areas in which you are ready to grow! And recognizing the personality types of others—realizing, for example, your key customer is more of a Miss Piggy than a Mr. Spock, will help you make a more dynamic connection.

How to recognize and connect with each personality type

The following descriptions are of "prototype" personalities. The majority of the people you work with will seldom exhibit such clear-cut tendencies. But these examples should highlight the key traits of the personality types to help you in identifying them in others.

The Determined personality

The Determined individual likes to be in charge. The Determined personality tends to exhibit the following characteristics:

- Cool, impersonal and in control.
- Readily disclose expectations.
- Results-oriented.
- Bottom-line-focused.
- Risk-taking.
- Competitive.
- Time-conscious.
- Goal-oriented.
- Gets things done and makes things happen.
- Poor listening skills.
- Impatient.
- Opinionated.

Determined personalities often gravitate toward careers as stockbrokers, independent consultants, corporate CEOs or drill sergeants. Examples of Determined people in politics, business and entertainment are former Great Britain Prime Minister Margaret Thatcher, Donald Trump and talk show host Oprah Winfrey.

You'll recognize the office of a Determined personality by a number of clues: The seating is formal, with guest chairs in front of the neat and organized desk. The desk may even be up on a platform, guests sitting on the lower level in chairs dwarfed by the size of the chair behind the desk. You generally won't see a jar of candy, personal mementos, clipped-out cartoons or family photos on the desk of the Determined professional. The decor suggests power. On the walls may be large planning calendars with deadlines and goals clearly displayed. Industry awards and honors are proudly displayed.

Connecting with the Determined personality

To make a more dynamic connection with a Determined personality, get to the point! Offer concise explanations—and focus on outcome rather than process. Whether a customer, co-worker or boss, this individual wants to know the bottom line: "How is this going to benefit me?" "What's it going to cost me?" "How much money will we save?" "When will this project be completed?"

Don't talk to Determineds about personal development issues—especially theirs! They don't appreciate your getting too close. Suggest ideas for business strategies instead. Don't use pointless humor or engage in small talk ("How was your weekend?"). Stay focused on the topic at hand. Determineds do not want to know the long process used to arrive at your conclusion. Sum up the situation and conclude with a call for action—one that they can delegate!

When preparing a report for a Determined boss, be concise: one or two pages tops. When faxing to a Determined business associate, eliminate the extraneous cover page. When looking for ways to reach the Determined customer, consider promoting speedy service, bottom-line savings and solid, no-hassle guarantees.

The Instinctive personality

The Instinctive individual is more of a people person. He or she leads with emotions and values relationships. The Instinctive personality is typically:

- Open.
- Receptive.
- Unassuming.
- Reliable and loyal.
- Steady worker.

- Excellent team player.
- Slow to make decisions.
- Not time-conscious.
- Tends to generalize.
- Supportive of others.
- Seeks close, first-name basis relationships.
- Avoids high-risk situations.

Instinctives are often found in careers like counseling, teaching, social work, the ministry, psychology, nursing or human resource development. Examples of such personalities are TV's June Cleaver ("Leave it to Beaver"), newswoman Mary Richards ("The Mary Tyler Moore Show") and Barbara Bush.

Instinctives like those types of warm commercials on TV showing a family going to a restaurant where the waitress gives a toy to the smiling child. Those are the images these people are persuaded by. More than most, they like to feel that their families are warm, safe and happy. These sorts of ideas and images make more of an impact on the Instinctives than they would on other personality types.

How can you tell if a person is an Instinctive when you walk into his or her office? You'll see pictures of family and other personal items—perhaps a jar of candy—on the desk. The walls have personal slogans, which hang next to more family pictures. The ambience is friendly. Often, the seating is more informal, guest chairs not separated from the occupant's chair by a desk. Perhaps a "family room" arrangement, with sofa, chairs and coffee table substitutes for the more formal desk-and-chairs layout.

Connecting with the Instinctive personality

If you must present information to an Instinctive, dump the heavily detailed charts. Instinctives don't learn as easily from graphs, charts or long, involved discussions of statistics. While everyone needs some logic to persuade them, the Instinctives don't need as much. What they *do* need more than most is the ability to relate to and trust you. You'll convince these people more effectively with an informal, conversational approach or a group discussion.

Instinctives thrive on contact. Close friends, loyal long-term customers and clients and, when appropriate, even friendly co-workers will be open to warm handshakes, back-patting and even hugs.

A few persuasive words Instinctives learn by are: *nice, compatible, comfortable, user-friendly, warm, trust, participation* and *teamwork.*

When you are connecting with an Instinctive customer, the personal touch goes a long way. This individual will be comfortable opening up his or her protective territory to allow you to stand closer. He or she responds well to food and gifts. A gift basket makes a great follow-up thank-you, for example. The Instinctive customer will also respond well to interest in his or her children or family.

Instinctive workers often function better when they are part of a team. While they don't enjoy the spotlight, they do like working with and helping others. In meetings with Instinctives, it helps to open with some small talk—"How was everyone's weekend?"—and conclude by thanking individuals for their commitment and support.

The Visionary personality

The Visionary is focused on detail and concerned with the analytical process. This individual tends to concentrate more on the means rather than the end. He or she is very logical and very thorough. Other common characteristics of the Visionary include:

- Reserved.
- Slower to make decisions.
- Self-contained.
- Good at working at solitary tasks.
- Good at problem-solving.
- Learns best by reading.
- Hates to be wrong.
- Avoids taking risks.
- Logical and methodical.

Visionaries are often found in such careers as quality control, accounting, engineering, computer programming, architecture, systems analysis, dentistry—and other technical and hard science professions. Examples of this type are Mr. Spock of "Star Trek" and Ralph Nader.

If you walk into the office of a Visionary, you see a desk covered with neat piles of charts and graphs. Walls, as well, may be covered with evidence of his or her work. Don't expect to find much in the way of personal expression. There will be few family photos or decorative touches. Where is the chair for the visitor placed? The question is not where—but if there's a chair at all. This type is task-oriented, focused on work, not entertaining visitors to the office. If there is a guest chair, it will likely be placed across the desk, possibly even against the far wall of the office.

Connecting with the Visionary personality

Whether you're confronted with a Visionary employee, boss or customer, you're not going to persuade these people to do anything if you haven't first given them a great wealth of information. Your Visionary customer will want to see how-to manuals, product ratings and consumer reviews before making a purchasing decision. Your Visionary supervisor will want to see reports, data and a thorough proposal before he or she approves your recommendation. Your Visionary employee will ask for charts, graphs and other background information before feeling comfortable with moving forward with a new project.

Visionaries learn well by reading, so give them as much background and support materials as you can. And be prepared to spend time explaining exactly what you want them to do—and how to do it. They find it difficult to make decisions if you don't give them a detailed process to follow. The pace of the Visionary is likely to be slower than others. Visionary purchasers may take longer to part with their money, bosses slower in giving their approval.

Normally, visionaries do not welcome physical contact unless they invite it. Avoid back-slapping, arm-touching and other gestures that may be acceptable to other personality types, and limit such contact to formal handshakes.

Each personality type has certain language they respond to more positively. The Visionary hears you better when you use terms like: *precise, classified, quantified, qualified, logical, reasoned, facts, specific, figures, trials, tested* and *proven.*

The Enthusiastic personality

Enthusiastics are the flamboyant and emotional types. As the name implies, they are happiest and most productive when they can embrace their jobs with passion and excitement. They are not averse to being in the spotlight, and enjoy contact with others. Enthusiastics exhibit the following traits:

- Relationship-oriented.
- Open and direct.
- Creative.
- Crave attention and enjoy being in the spotlight.
- Need support from others.
- Make quick decisions.
- Risk-takers.
- Dream-chasers.
- Not time-conscious.
- Tend to generalize and exaggerate.
- Respond emotionally rather than logically.

You find Enthusiastics in glamorous, high-profile careers, such as sales, public relations, trial law and, of course, acting. Examples of Enthusiastics are Miss Piggy, Jonathan Winters, Dr. Ruth Westheimer and Johnnie Cochran.

The office of an Enthusiastic personality may be cluttered and disorganized. The walls may be covered with inspiring posters expressing motivational slogans. The arrangement may be open and friendly, with seating arranged so people can talk easily (of course!). Our Enthusiastic wants as many people as possible in the office. Chairs— plural—are arranged in a group setting. On the desk are toys and fun things to entertain people.

Connecting with the Enthusiastic personality

Enthusiastics love the opportunity to talk and perform. Don't bore them with the processes, and detailed facts and figures. They don't want to hear it. Straight lecture doesn't bear much fruit with these people. They don't want to listen—they want a high level of involvement and interaction. They want bells and whistles. If you are selling to an Enthusiastic, make your presentation even more fun than usual—and involve the customer. Let him or her open doors, hold the product or test it out. Get him or her excited.

In meetings, let your Enthusiastic people have an opportunity to lead or present, but give them a time limit. Ask for an outline in advance (typically, Enthusiastics will prefer to "wing it").

If you work with a sales staff, consider some fun incentives and unique ways to offer recognition. I once worked with an Enthusiastic who loved to hand out cigars and slap backs whenever he made a big sale. I went one further: I brought in a large, brass nautical bell that could be heard throughout the entire office building when rang. The salespeople got to ring the bell each time they made a big sale. My highly Enthusiastic salesman lit up each time he got to ring the bell. I lit up, too. Sales increased and so did motivation.

Involving Instinctives and Visionaries

The more reserved Instinctives and Visionaries often withdraw from communicating in a group situation or meeting. They may be reluctant to speak out or express their thoughts in a sales situation. When they are being quiet as mice, it's easy to look the other way and plow ahead with your own agenda. Don't! Instead, find ways to gently allow them to express themselves. Instinctives and Visionaries often have a great deal of knowledge and valuable input, though they may be uncomfortable volunteering it.

If you come bounding up to Instinctives or Visionaries like a "wild and crazy guy," with a noisemaker and party hat, you are going to scare them. Start off in a calm, less threatening manner. Soften your voice and use modest gestures. Once you get them warmed up and trust has been built, you can try more expressive communication.

When you pose a question, give them a few seconds. These types take much longer to think through answers. Phrase it this way, "Let's both take a moment to think up some ideas about that. I am going to write mine down, it helps me think." This gives them permission—with honor—to take the time they need to process. When the time comes, they'll feel more comfortable about sharing. They won't feel inadequate because they took longer to come up with an answer.

If you want to encourage their participation in meetings, give them warning prior to the meeting so that they can prepare. During the meeting, you may have to run interference with the more assertive Determineds and Enthusiastics who may be tempted to interrupt or take over these more soft-spoken individuals.

Reining in Determineds and Enthusiastics

If you don't take charge of these personality types, they might take charge of everything! Because they're expressive and outgoing, they have a tendency to dominate a conversation or meeting.

Make sure you give them an opportunity to hold the floor. These types don't listen if you don't give them the public attention they crave. When you feel they've had a fair amount of time, conclude their presentation by acknowledging their contribution and thanking them.

Don't expect this type to suffer through a long meeting or presentation from you. They stop listening if they sit too long. Get them moving; put them to work. They are doers, so give them something to do. In a sales situation, for example, allow your Determined or Enthusiastic customer to try out the product.

Adapting your style to others

Wouldn't it be nice if all of our customers had a sign around their necks saying, "Pick me! Easy to work with! High Profit margin!"? Or that all potential employees had signs that communicated "Guaranteed loyal, hardworking employee that will be the perfect fit for your company." Alas, despite the clues you now have for identifying different personality types, there is no 100-percent way to predict exactly how you'll get along with a particular client or co-worker. And, of course, even if you could, you often don't have a choice in whom you work with. Because of this, you need to be able to *adapt* your style to the personality styles of others in order to most effectively connect with them.

Last year I began working with a company consisting of a group of distributors. Each distributor has, as all individuals do, his or her own personality. One distributor had a particularly strong Determined personality—and his reputation had preceded him. People respected him as highly intelligent, but he was known as dominant and driven, the classic Determined personality.

During a break at his company's national convention, an individual walked up, offered his hand and introduced himself to me. It was *him*! The dominant and driven one! I didn't know whether to be thrilled or horrified. The worst thing you can do with a classic Determined personality such as this is to let him see you flinch. He asked for my card and said he might want to speak with me when the convention was over regarding possibly training his group. I responded with "I'd be happy to *exchange* business cards with you. I believe I have some time to meet with you tomorrow." (In reality I had all day free. It was either him or the beach—we were in Florida.)

He came to the meeting the next day. It was there I discovered one more reason why this powerful and Determined person is an overwhelming success! The other half of his business team came to the meeting—his wife! She has all the best qualities of the Instinctive, which makes an incredible balance. We qualified and questioned each other and left the meeting with an agreement for two scheduled days, one consultative and one for training services.

I thought it would be smooth sailing from there, now that I had used my communication skills to make a dynamic connection with him. But, in all of our dealings, he was still the dominant Determined. For example, during our next meeting he was explaining how the geographical and demographic differences of his area contrasted to others. I responded with: "I'm familiar with that area, I have a relative who lives near there." He would respond with something like: "That's fine but that's not what we are here to discuss."

He prides himself on working me harder and longer than the others in the group. He lets me know that is what he expects. He may not realize yet that I am enough of a Determined professional and person overall, that I am driven on every job I do! But I am enough of an Instinctive professional to allow him to think it is his idea!

Recently, however, I was pleasantly surprised with one of our interactions. I met with that same group of distributors again. I had numerous goals for that encounter: My first goal was to explain the sales presentation guide and the sales script I had assisted his company in developing. Second was to thank people for their assistance on the project. Third was to provide additional training for the majority of groups represented in that room. I believe my friend, the dominant and driven one, sensed my third goal. Although prior to the start of the meeting he had already booked one day of training, near the end of the meeting he jumped in unexpectedly with, "Okay, Laura, we'd like you to come down for three days—when is the soonest you can make it?"

Now, I don't think my friend would ever admit it, but his Instinctive side wanted to help me. As a leader in that group, he knew the actions he and his wife took would be emulated by most of the group. He was correct. Most of the distributors present that day booked me. I also believe that my friend would rather that I hadn't figured this out. But I did. Thank you, Henry.

I was able to use my Instincts to determine the personality types of Henry and his wife. This information allowed me to set my pace to match theirs and gave me the opportunity to make a dynamic connection. This important connection turned into numerous training days as well as a new friendship.

Career Profile Assessments

I recommend that any individual who is hiring, even when highly trained at hiring, use a Career Profile Assessment to assist in identifying the ideal candidates for the position. Career Profile Assessments identify different character traits and the levels of those traits that may be important to the position for which an individual is being considered. Some of the character traits that the assessment measures include discipline, stability, extroversion, independence, creativity, entrepreneurism and assertiveness.

Some of the Career Profiles, such as the ones my company provides, are developed by occupational psychologists and include validity indicators to help verify the accuracy of the results. The assessment includes a narrative report that discusses the individual's personality in detail and how it may apply to business. The greatest benefit of this assessment is to provide an objective insight to weigh your own assessment against. It should *not* be used exclusively to make hiring, terminating or promoting decisions.

Although the career profile my company offers is not solely an integrity test, some factors can offer an insight into possible hostilities. In my consulting career, I have been informed that numerous potentially negative hiring and or promotional decisions have been avoided because of information provided by a career profile. Additionally, many worthy professionals have been promoted because of such an assessment. The enlightening results prove well worth the modest investment.

While working with a new client, I recommended that his company use a Career Profile Assessment for hiring and, in addition, conduct one for all of their existing employees. When the reports were computed, there was one that was alarming. This individual's report indicated that his stability level was extremely low and his assertive and nonconforming levels were extremely high. Within days of the scoring, and before the employer was able to meet with the employee to discuss the profile and coach the individual, the employee began screaming and throwing things at a customer and had to be removed from the property. In contrast, when an opening in management became available, we gave Career Profile Assessments to all of the candidates who asked for consideration. The individual who was hired showed quite a few strengths that were conducive to the position. In addition, the career profile indicated some minor possible deficiencies that were able to be emphasized during training.

Handwriting analysis or graphology

Handwriting analysis is another method of discovering clues to whom you're dealing with. The information you learn from an individual's handwriting will provide you with valuable information about how best to connect with him or her.

I first became interested in handwriting analysis when an employer asked me to take an occupational assessment test that included handwriting analysis. I was skeptical, but was absolutely amazed with the accuracy of the results. Since then I have read numerous books on *graphology* or handwriting analysis. I find it extremely helpful in understanding the people with whom I am striving to connect.

Skeptical? Like medicine, graphology is based on empirical study. In other words, thousands of samples were evaluated to determine like patterns and similar traits before rendering conclusions. Researchers discovered similar characteristics that corresponded to graphological patterns in writing. In Western Europe, graphology is studied extensively at leading universities and is considered accurate by many world-respected employers.

I was fascinated to learn that studies have shown that people who have become paralyzed are able to recreate their original handwriting by writing with a pen held by their feet or mouths. That is because all of our external movements are governed by neurological impulses that come from the brain. An angry man will write with an angry hand, thus, it is easy to determine if you have an angry employee. People can often hide negative traits in a well-rehearsed job interview. However, a person's basic nature will surface in his or her handwriting.

After a brief analysis of a complete stranger's handwriting, a graphologist can correctly determine characteristics reflected in it. A graphologist can correctly assess personality traits, including leadership skills, integrity and work habits.

Who uses graphology? Couples on the brink of matrimony, employers evaluating employees, attorneys assessing possible jurors, psychologists assessing children with possible attention deficit disorder (ADD), and the list goes on.

I am confident that handwriting analysis will provide employers with major assistance even more in the near future. Professionals claim they can detect an exaggerated temper, addictive traits, honesty, energy levels and intelligence. Personnel studies indicate that only 11 out of 100 employees will be at the same job five years after being hired. At an average training cost of between $35,000 and $50,000, it is critical to make excellent choices while hiring.

Handwriting analysis can also increase your knowledge of your customers. It has certainly helped me. Here are a few tips that I have found most helpful. However, please remember that just because you see one example of a particular trait, don't assume that this accurately reflects the individual. For example, if one "i" is dotted with a circle rather than a dot, but all the other "i's" feature dots, then the most frequently used style reflects the dominant trait.

Slant. The direction, or slant, the handwriting takes is an indication of how much control a person has over his or her emotions. Slant can help you differentiate between a logical, level-headed decision-maker or an emotionally charged, top-producing salesman.

- A backhand or upright position indicates a person who is cool, logical and in control of his or her emotions. The more forward the handwriting is slanted, the more the individual is ruled by emotions.

- A far left slant indicates a person who is extremely private.

- If I were looking for an outgoing, relationship-oriented person, I would look for writing with a forward slant.

- Writing that slants downhill indicates the writer is becoming low on energy and possibly may be depressed.

- An upward slant generally reflects a person who is more upbeat and positive.

- A severe uphill or downhill baseline indicates a person who doesn't have control of his or her feelings, whether sad or happy.

• When the slant is inconsistent, the individual may be inconsistent. This might be an indication of moodiness.

• Frequent slant changes indicates a person who may fluctuate in business decisions, perhaps being wildly enthusiastic to being noncommittal or even withdrawn.

Pressure. The pressure someone applies while writing can describe his or her supply of energy. The more pressure, the more energy at the time of writing.

• To discover a person's Determination in handwriting, look for very heavy pressure on the down strokes, such as the "y's" or "g's."

Spacing. The spacing of words and letters reflects whether the writer is a clear or confident thinker.

• When a person's handwriting is consistently and evenly spaced, this indicates a clarity of thought.

• Irregular pauses may indicate prolonged hesitation where a person has stopped to think about what he or she *should* be writing. Therefore, he or she may have paused to disguise or alter the truth or true thoughts.

• An exaggerated pause in writing, as in speaking, is a red flag that something may be amiss. More questioning on the issue would be well-advised.

   Consult with a professional graphologist before you make any decisions about a person's honesty and dishonesty.

Signature. There is an enormous misconception about the importance of the signature. Whereas your handwriting is an indication of who you really are, your signature reflects only what you want the world to *think* you are. It is a public persona created for the outside world.

Handwriting analysis is another method of exploration that will help you use your Instincts when connecting with people in your professional or personal life.

Mirroring and modeling

Santini and I in a behavior called "imitate." First Santini watches, then perfectly copies my movements.

Mirroring is a concept that has been interpreted by too many business people as, far too simplistically, copying the nonverbal and verbal cues of the person you're working with. In other words, if the individual smiles, *you* smile; if the individual scratches his or her head, *you* scratch *your* head. Warning: Don't take this too literally. If your customer is having a lousy day, you should act as if you're having a lousy day? If he's bored, you should act bored? Absolutely not!

One of the positive things about mirroring, however, is that it forces you to actually notice what the other person is doing. You should not mirror gestures or words that are based on insecurities and discomfort, though. You can make a customer feel secure and in safe waters without mirroring negative actions. (We will discuss this in greater detail in Dynamic Four: Enthusiasm.) Your job is to make a *dynamic* connection, not a dismal one.

Survey, and you will succeed!

As I have shown you so far, there are many ways to use your Instincts to encourage communication and explore the needs of others in your business dealings. One way to find out what your team and/or customers want, think and need is to listen to them! Many empires have been built because the leaders listened to their customers.

Years ago, as pizza restaurants grew in popularity, customers began complaining that it took too long to come in, order a pizza and drive it home for the family. Domino's listened, and offered guaranteed quick delivery.

In the past, in order to get those great vacation shots developed, you had to bring them to a drug store or photo developer, and then wait a week or more to get them back. Many people complained they couldn't stand waiting so long for their pictures to be developed. Well, someone listened. And now one-hour film developers flourish, many with convenient drive-through windows. And, yes, people are willing to pay extra for speedy service.

One excellent method of gathering information about what your customers want, like and don't like is to take a survey. This method works for *internal* customers—employees, vendors and consultants—as well, increasing their loyalty and making them feel important and valued because you asked for their opinion.

Some of the information you will receive from the survey will include a measurement of the quality of your service, the reliability of your merchandise, current and future trends, advertising effectiveness and the competitor's impact.

Distribution and returns for your survey

Depending on your resources and how much you want to spend, you can conduct your survey via mail, telephone or in person. I recommend the telephone whenever possible because it is inexpensive and highly efficient. If you choose the telephone, consider offering your customers an incentive such as a percentage off their next purchase as appreciation for their assistance. This is a great way to grab their attention in a positive way, and they're less likely to confuse the phone call with a solicitation. Normally by mail, you can expect between a 2-percent and 5-percent return. Recently, however, one large retailer I work with mailed 12,000 surveys out and received 1,200 responses back, an exceptional 10-percent return.

Why don't most businesses conduct customer surveys? The biggest reason: Owners and management are often afraid of the responses. In addition, they are a great deal of work (which is why they bring *us* in to coordinate them). But speaking from a great deal of experience, I've learned that they are not that difficult and are well worth the effort. Here are some of the benefits of customer surveys:

Benefit: Customer surveys assess your customer demographics, which can help target and maximize your advertising investment. By assessing your customer demographics you will be able to tell where to best invest in advertising dollars and special promotions. If you are drawing customers from a certain area of town where you do not have a location, consider working with a complementary type of business to gain exposure. You may want to exchange coupons to include in each other's mailings, particularly in thank-you cards. The coupons should not include a hook such as "Buy one, get one free." Instead, you should offer a percentage off, dollars off or completely free merchandise. The purpose is to get that person into your store.

Benefit: Customer surveys assess the effectiveness of your advertising. Let's say you have been advertising in a particular section of the newspaper and you want to determine if people are seeing it. A survey is a great way of identifying what percentage of your customers responded to that ad.

Benefit: A customer survey checks on the promptness and courtesy of a specific department. One company that conducted a customer survey found that customers didn't like the fact that the individuals on the delivery crew were not on time and didn't wipe their feet when they carried the merchandise into the customers' homes. Easy remedies were available and the company found customer satisfaction went up measurably after the remedies were applied.

One progressive furniture retailer found out from its survey that customers wanted the same instant gratification from a furniture purchase that they received in almost every other purchase they made—they wanted their new sofa or dining room set *immediately*. So the company now keeps its merchandise in stock and delivers to its customer the day they make their purchase. This gave the company an edge over the competition, not just in terms of delivery. Prospective and existing customers perceive this company as being in tune with their desires.

Benefit: A customer survey verifies that specials and add-ons are actually being promoted by sales staff. One of the reasons I had a higher-than-90-percent closing ratio of add-ons was because I simply told my customers about them in an enthusiastic manner. Why did I do that? Three reasons: I believed my customers would benefit from them, I wanted the bonus and I believed the owner of the company might check up on me. I'm not sure which motivated me more. Again, if a survey reveals that your salespeople are not mentioning add-ons, don't make anyone feel singled out—just deal with it as a way of checking on customer impressions.

Benefit: A customer survey provides you with specific employee performance information. This will build accountability and, therefore, escalate employee performance. Once an employee knows that you are paying attention to him or her, the individual will generally make every effort to do a better job. Most people want positive recognition. Let your employees know in advance that you are going to use a customer survey to stay on top of customers' impressions of the company. Do not make them think you are specifically checking on them.

Create your own surveys

Prepare a simple questionnaire of 12 to 15 questions. (Asking more questions than that will just annoy people.) Do not be afraid of the results. To give your customers reasons to buy from you, you must know what your customers want. It is critical for a company to take a long hard look at itself from time to time.

Sample of telephone survey for a women's clothing store

Customer name:_____

Date:_____

Address:_____

_____

Phone number:_____

1. How often do you shop for clothing for yourself?_____

_____

_____

2. How often do you shop at Inspiration Designs?_____

_____

_____

3. Where else do you shop for clothing for yourself?_____

_____

_____

4. What two adjectives would you use to describe Inspiration
Designs?_____

_____

5. What one adjective would you use to describe Inspiration
Designs' service?_____

6. Who generally takes care of you at Inspiration Designs?_____

_____

7. What additional merchandise would you like Inspiration
Designs to carry?_____

_____

_____

8. How much do you estimate you spend on clothing for yourself
annually?_____

_____

9. What percentage of that do you estimate you spend at Inspiration Designs?_____

10. What adjectives would you use to describe our price points?____

11. What advertising source used by Inspiration Designs catches your attention the most?_____

12. What can Inspiration Designs do to make your shopping experience more enjoyable?_____

13. What do you like the most about Inspiration Designs?_____

14. Do you work inside or out of the home?
   ❑ In   ❑ Out

15. What is your occupation?_____

16. What is your age category?
   ❑ 18-25   ❑ 26-40   ❑ 41-55   ❑ 56 and over

External customer surveys should:

- Measure your customer demographics.
- Maximize your advertising investment.
- Verify the effectiveness of your advertising.
- Check on the promptness and courtesy of specific departments.
- Verify that specials and add-ons are being promoted by your sales staff.
- Provide you with additional specific employee performance information.

Survey secrets

- Where appropriate, use open-ended questions that require more than a yes or no response.
- Have an enthusiastic, friendly person who is well-trained make the phone calls.
- Have a log to track the results.
- Start with 50 to 100 of your most recent customers who have received your products or services. This way you can gather information on the entire sales process.
- The best calling time is generally between 6:30 p.m. to 8:30 p.m., Monday through Friday.

For a sample survey, to help get you thinking about how to design your own, see pages 104 and 105. I designed and conducted this telephone survey for a progressive clothing store—Inspiration Designs, in Rochester, New York.

Reward your customers' participation

Any behavior you want repeated should be rewarded (this is called *shaping*). Because feedback from your customers is vital, reward them when they give it regardless of whether it is positive or negative. Frankly, the negative feedback is generally much more valuable. In

Sample Internal Customer Survey

1. What do you like most about working for ABC Company?

_____
_____
_____
_____
_____
_____

2. What do you dislike most about working for ABC Company?

_____
_____
_____
_____
_____
_____

3. What suggestions, if any, do you have to improve the working environment?

_____
_____
_____
_____
_____
_____

4. How long have you been with the company?

❑ less than 1 year   ❑ 1-3 years   ❑ 4-9 years
❑ 10 or more years

(optional)

Name: _____
Department:_____

addition to offering them incentives such as coupons or discounts when you conduct the survey, send a thank-you letter and call to let them know how you are following up on their ideas.

When surveying internal customers

An internal customer survey is just as important as an external customer survey in today's shark-infested business waters. Without happy employees, chances are you won't have happy customers. The sample survey on page 107 is another Instinctive way to gather information from internal customers in order for you to make a stronger connection.

Obviously, if you see some trends in attitude among your internal customers, you can assume there is some validity. For example, if 75 percent of the company employees are saying they would like more feedback about their work performance, you should evaluate your performance appraisal process and look for other ways to offer such feedback.

Instinctive listening and questioning skills

Having excellent listening skills does not mean simply *hearing* others. It means hearing the message behind the words, translating that message along with the nonverbal messages you pick up with your Instinctive sonar. Questioning and listening are important because they tell your customers you are interested in them. The best kind of questions to ask are questions about your customers' interests, desires, experiences, expectations and preferences.

Through Instinctive, disciplined listening you will be able to let your customers know, "I'm interested, I'm listening and I'm on your side." *Sharks* and fools may often interrupt a customer, talk over a client or finish a customer's sentences. They will probably give other indications of poor listening skills: waiting for an individual to finish, then launching into their own agendas, for example.

A *dolphin*, on the other hand, picks up on the *feelings* of others, as well as their words. He or she may take notes, if necessary, or make other efforts to get information that's important to the customer. A dolphin will smile, establish and maintain appropriate eye contact and nod his or her head as the individual is speaking.

A dolphin or a shark? A dolphin of course!

The best way to be an Instinctive listener is to be a good explorer and questioner. A great communicator is one who listens and watches carefully, then asks the appropriate question, and listens again. When you ask great questions (particularly open-ended questions—discussed later in this section) you will get information that will help you connect.

When you are with a customer, before you start asking any questions, stop a moment and connect with your Instincts. Wait for your Instincts to advise you on the best way to connect with this person. I don't mean wait minutes—I mean wait a second or two. Often your silence will be thought of as brilliant and wise and will encourage them to communicate.

The question *not* to ask

As I mentioned earlier, I do not recommend asking your customer "How much would you like to spend?" or "What price range did you have in mind?" Here's why: A customer will almost always respond with an amount at the lowest end of the product line—or lower than realistic. Why? Because when asked, the customer perceives the price is open to negotiation. Now, the salesperson must convince the customer to spend more money than he or she has committed to verbally. The customer "owns" those words and feels he or she must stick to them.

The same is true for budgets. If they have a budget they must stay within and you go over it, they will tell you. This is far better than the customer making a decision solely based on price and receiving inferior products or services. Customers generally do not base their buying decision solely on price.

I hope you will never again ask, "How much you would like to spend?" or "What is your budget for this?" as you are working on forming a dynamic connection with a customer. Instead, by your gentle use of more effective questions, you will uncover pertinent needs and benefits that the customer may not have even considered. The customer will generally appreciate your interest and follow your advice regarding the best product.

Be careful with closed-ended questions

Questions that can be answered with either a yes or no will most frequently be answered with a no by your customers because they are uncomfortable in your territory. They are simply responding defensively. In order to make the most of closed-ended questions, choose your words carefully to elicit a *positive* response. In other words, you want to ask yes questions. Yes questions also encourage customers to verbally express and confirm their interest, both to you and themselves. Some great yes questions include:

- "Is it important for you to deal with a company and with products that are proven and reliable?"
- "Is quality something that is important to you?"

- "Do you like the fact that we are the highest recommended widget company in the country?"
- "Do you like the fact that we offer a 100-percent satisfaction guarantee?"

Get the most from open-ended questions

My favorite question of all is the open-ended question—the type that requires more than a yes or no answer. An open-ended question is designed to get customers to give more information about their desires and about themselves overall. The more information they give you, the better your chances are for a strong relationship and, therefore, obtaining an agreement. An open-ended question typically begins with *who, what, where, when, why* and *how.*

Say, you're a salesperson at a mattress company. Some great questions to ask during the qualification stage might include:

- "What kind of mattress do you have now?"
- "What made you decide to replace it?"
- "What did you like about it?"
- "What don't you like about your current mattress?"

Now think about the answers that go with these questions. "Well, it's an ABC brand." You respond with a nod. This great question has begun to position you as an expert, you will seem to know so many brands. "It's 10 years old, a spring is coming through." Your customer has just began creating a strong sense of urgency. The best part of this is, later in the presentation, you will be able to use information that your prospective customer has offered to show the importance of your products and or services as reasons to make a purchasing decision today.

Her are more examples of open-ended questions:

- "What most interests you about _____?"
- "How familiar are you with _____?"
- "What great things have you heard about (our company) or (our product)?"
- "What brought you in today?"

- "What can I do to help you?"
- "Where may I direct you?"
- "How may we be of assistance?"
- "What did you like most about what you are currently using, driving, etc.?"
- "What do you dislike about what you are currently using?"
- "What can we do to make this work better?"
- "What key results are you looking for?"
- "What do you do for a living?"

As the dynamic communicator, you must be prepared to lead. Many people are just too shy, nervous and uninformed to ask questions. Often they feel their own questions may be potentially silly or embarrassing, or they simply might not think of them. If you are Instinctive, you can plant questions in their minds that will help them communicate and give you the tools you need to assist them. Unless important information is uncovered, they may not accept or even fully understand the benefits of your product or service.

Consider questions that many of your customers ask, and prepare responses that will be simple and make them feel comfortable. I suggest you actually write out these responses so you can effectively practice and rehearse them.

By telling your current customers what other customers wanted to know, you are building their curiosity and, therefore, building interest in an area. These prompting responses can also help you through any lulls in a conversation. I begin my statement with, "A lot of people are curious about whether....Was that something you were interested in knowing?" Often they will say something like "Why, yes, I was." Or maybe they will say, "No, what I was wondering was..." or "Yes, I was just going to ask that!" (If they say no, and nothing more, smile and move on to another question.) Here are some examples of questions that will elicit customer involvement:

- "Were you looking for a particular color?"
- "Were you interested in our current specials?"
- "How might you use that?"
- "What have you heard about that/it?"

- "How would it be useful?"
- "What has been your experience with it before?"
- "What other applications could you use this for?"
- "Is the reputation of the company you are dealing with important to you?"

Can you ask too many questions?

It is very rare that you could ask too many questions, if you ask them with interest rather than with an interrogational tone. My rule is the more questions the better. Especially if they are smart questions.

My friend Dottie Walters, a pioneer of women in sales, is today a brilliant professional speaker. I love to hear her tell a story of Sarah Bernhardt. Dottie says that in *all* encounters, "interested" is irresistible. When the great nineteenth-century stage actress Sarah Bernhardt lost her leg in an accident, she bravely continued her career on the stage. When her theatrical company arrived at a new city, a newspaper editor told a young reporter to interview her. He didn't want to go. He said, "She is a has-been—ugly, old!" He went very reluctantly. But when he came back, he sat down and began to write a glowing story about the actress. The savvy editor asked the young man, "What did you and Sarah Bernhardt talk about?" The young reporter replied, "Come to think of it, she didn't say much. But every time I said something, she leaned forward with a smile, looked into my eyes, and said, 'And then?' "

"Be more interested than interesting."
—Dottie Walters

I had the honor of speaking with a remarkable lady recently. She told me an interesting story. Several years ago, on her birthday, she went to the local automobile dealership for some information about a car she liked. She asked the salesman to discuss the car, but he looked at her as if questioning that she could afford it. The salesman responded condescendingly, and said, "It has four wheels, an engine and it's black and white." Keeping her mood in check (after all it was her birthday), she asked, "Well, I'd like to talk to your manager then, please:" "Sure, he's at lunch, you can come back later."

Now she had an hour to kill. She took herself—and her purse filled with the cash to pay for the car in full—over to the dealer next door to "window shop." She stood there gazing at a beautiful new model, sadly thinking it was way beyond the goal she had set. A young man came over to her and began to gently question her needs. Still feeling the sting from the other dealership's treatment, she revealed to this attentive salesperson, "It's my birthday." He wished her a happy birthday and quickly excused himself. Before too long his secretary returned and he presented her with a dozen roses!

Yes, she bought the car from the "interested" salesman! He helped her work out the terms. Mary Kay Ash, of Mary Kay Cosmetics is today quite famous for the many cars her company buys. Something tells me she never went back to that first dealership to buy a single one! The second salesperson showed genuine interest in Mary Kay and the result was a dynamic connection and a new client. Asking the right questions in the right way will give you the information you need to make a dynamic connection with your customer.

Addressing and understanding individual needs

The Instinctive salesman in the Mary Kay story was able to connect with his customer by showing sincere interest. Your questions and Instinctive listening will help you understand other people's desires. Remember, people make connections and commitments because they want to. Make them want to connect with you. It is *your* job.

When you determine what someone's desire is, you can and should address your comments to that level. If your goal is to persuade or motivate others to act, you must first determine where they are now. Then (and only then!) can you connect with them and motivate them to act.

Recently, I consulted with a client whose employee was taking off from work too much. This employee had performed well overall for the two years he was with the company. However, recently he had repeatedly asked for a few hours off each week. Rather than blast him regarding his unacceptable behavior, we first questioned and then observed his answers and realized something was deeply troubling him.

A few days later, we showed up at a service call he was working on. Helping him finish the job a little quicker gave us an opportunity to talk. I began by sincerely complimenting a few aspects of his performance. This, combined with the attention and time spent assisting him on the call, seemed to help him open up. I then asked him how things were going with the job, how he was enjoying it. He said he was enjoying work all right. The tone in his voice, however, said that something else was *not* all right. I responded with a curious, "Well, how's everything else going?" He went on to tell me his wife was having trouble with her pregnancy. He was taking time off to take her to doctors.

By letting him know that we would like to help him during a difficult time, he felt he had a partner rather than an enemy. We spent a few minutes discussing his situation and then I explained my expectations. We came up with alternatives such as mostly using off hours to schedule his wife's appointments. I realized, however, his mind would not be fully on his job if he was worried about his wife. I knew my client had a pager in the office that was not in use so I volunteered to give it to him and asked him to give his wife the number so she could reach him in case of an emergency.

We ended the meeting with me converting our agreements to writing and he signed off that he understood them and agreed. The result? An employee who felt that he was supported, and who understood there were guidelines that needed to be respected. By understanding this individual's needs, we were able to motivate him to focus on his work by making him feel comfortable that his wife could reach him at any time.

When someone steps over a well-clarified line, you need to react in a cool, respectful and firm way, explaining that the behavior (not the person) is unacceptable. We will examine this further in "Employee discipline: how, when and why," later in this section.

In another situation, I was coaching a salesperson on an in-home presentation. By observing both the salesperson and the customer closely, I noticed that the customer was exhausted. It is never wise to say, "Boy, you look terrible." Through questioning I uncovered that the husband had just returned from Japan on business and had not slept in more than a day. I considered my choices: I could reschedule, plow ahead or acknowledge his situation. I chose the latter and responded, "Well, let me go through this a little more briefly than I usually do so that I can let you get to sleep." He seemed to very much appreciate my concern. And, yes, we obtained the sale that night.

Again, by using my sonar and tuning into this individual's needs, I was able to motivate him to focus on my presentation, and ultimately led him to make a purchase. Understanding personal needs will help you connect more dynamically.

Reading commitment signals

Using your Instincts to connect with customers includes knowing when you've made a connection—and when they are ready to buy. If you are in any business that involves sales, this skill alone will increase your wealth. To do this you need to watch what your customer's body is saying. Listen, question, listen some more and continue to watch. Eventually, you will hear or see the message, "I am ready to commit." When you see or hear a buying signal, it's time to obtain the sale.

Your customer may exhibit cues or signs of readiness to purchase, which may either be verbal responses or nonverbal expressions. When you witness one or more of the following, be prepared to respond and assist the process along. It may be a simple matter of taking down information, writing up the order and making arrangements for delivery.

Verbal signs of commitment

- "What is the warranty on this?"
- "Do you have it in stock?"
- "What is the delivery time?"
- "How long does it take you to install?"
- "How many do you have in stock?"
- "But I was hoping for one in blue."

- "I would need it delivered by Tuesday."
- "Is this the last one?"
- "What credit cards do you accept?"
- "Do you have financing?"
- "I like it."
- "I would need to wait until _____."

Nonverbal signs of commitment

- Customer nods head or smiles in agreement.
- Customer asks for a pen.
- Customer leans forward.
- Customer clasps and rubs hands together.
- Customer turns to companion (or you) as if seeking reassurance or permission.
- Customer takes physical possession of product or paperwork.

Have a commitment? Don't just stand there!

When a customer says, "What credit cards do you accept?" don't just stand there, obtain the sale! I am amazed when I hear salespeople respond with "Visa, MasterCard, and Discover" and then just stand there! The reply should be, "We accept Visa, MasterCard, and Discover. Which would you prefer to use today?" You answered the question; you connected to their desires; everyone is happy.

Once you see, hear or sense your customer's commitment, confirm agreement by saying something like, "Great, let's move over here so I can wrap up a few details for you," or "Great! I just have a few last questions for you." When your questions or details are worked out, hand the customer a pen and wrap it up.

How about in a nonsales situation—can you still find verbal and nonverbal signals for commitment? Let's say you have an employee who is causing some trouble with other employees. You decide to meet with the employee to clarify your expectations with him or her. After a few minutes into your meeting you observe that the employee seems to understand your position. Don't just stand there. Obtain agreement by converting your thoughts to writing and have the employee sign a sheet that he or she has read and agreed with the information.

Tips for dealing with difficult people

Exploration of desires is easier with some people than with others. Sometimes your Instinctive search to make a dynamic connection is thwarted by someone who is just plain difficult. We all need to deal with people who are difficult. Some days, they seem to prey on us like sharks! Exploring for information with someone in a rotten mood can test your Instinctive skills to the limit. But I have a few ideas that will help make it a bit easier.

What is a "difficult" person? It varies depending upon each situation. For example, a whining, complaining or rude individual might be considered "difficult" in most situations. Another might be the quiet and pleasant account representative who doesn't report any challenges with clients because he or she doesn't do enough troubleshooting.

When these individuals cause difficulties for you, it's important for you to realize that while you may not be able to control their behavior, you *can* control your attitude and response to their behavior. And that is your most powerful weapon in dealing with difficult people. *If you think that you will be able to resolve the issue, most likely you will.* If you think simply that this customer is a pain in the neck and nothing you do will make him or her happy, I guarantee you will have an unpleasant situation on your hands. Remember, I believe customers can "hear" what you're thinking, through their own Instinctive sonar!

If someone is causing you to be upset, really, what are your choices?

- Remain upset.
- Try to stop them from making you upset.
- Stop being upset yourself.

Yes, you only have one choice—to stop being upset yourself.

Six steps to diffuse emotional encounters

There are six steps to help diffuse emotional encounters. Let's go over each of them carefully.

Step 1. Prepare yourself. When a customer is rude and obnoxious, or a boss attacks your work, your gut reaction may be to fight back. Dolphins don't do that, sharks do. Instead, when you feel a challenging encounter begin, you need to take hold of your primitive and very natural Instinct to *defend* and instead allow your intellect to control you. To prepare yourself, keep open body language, adjust your posture so you are sitting or standing straight and have a pleasant, "I'm interested and want to help" smile. You need to feel and express overall alertness and attentiveness. The impression you should convey is that you are interested, concerned and ready to take action.

Step 2. Listen. As I discussed before, it can be hard to stay calm while you are under attack. But, for step two, listen objectively! For that you must stay calm.

Visualize the angry individual as a huge balloon—filled with too much air. Your listening rationally helps let that air out slowly. The more the person talks and the more you continue to listen, more and more air releases, and finally, it's all gone! Now you can finish the negotiations. The Instinctive skill you need to work on is in getting the air to release instead of increase.

Most of the time, the frustrated person just wants to feel somebody is listening. As he or she vents anger, imagine all that air slowly releasing. The more air is released, the closer you are to being able to help.

You encourage the individual to continue the diffusing process as you provide feedback, using reassuring body language such as nodding your head or expressing concern. Ask questions when possible to show you are listening and that you understand.

If you give them the chance, people will often talk themselves into your point of view. Dottie Walters bases most of her tremendous multi-million-dollar successes on the phrase, "Tell me about it." Try something like this: "Mr. Smith, I am very sorry for any misunderstanding. Please, would you tell me about it?"

Step 3. Establish rapport. Once that big balloon has run out of air (you have allowed the individual's emotions to run their course), you are ready to have a rational discussion. After all, discussion consisting mainly of hostile "oh yeah?" responses is really not very productive! Solutions come from rational discussion. Establishing rapport helps you build a bridge from the emotional to the rational discussion.

Tips to help establish rapport

- Always use positive body language, such as open-hand gestures and smiling or showing concern.
- Nod your head while your customer is speaking to show you are interested and on his or her side.
- Listen carefully to your customer. Never interrupt or become defensive.
- Use the individual's name when talking to him or her.
- Apologize for any confusion, miscommunication or inconvenience the situation might have caused.
- State your purpose, which is to solve the situation. Try not to call it a "problem," it just makes it seem worse. Use words such as *challenge*, *situation* or even *opportunity*.
- Take notes. It shows you care.
- Ask questions to gain clarification. Do not ask questions to dispute the individual's point of view, but only to clarify.
- Agree whenever you can. You will be amazed at all the things you can agree on in an argument. Look for them and use them. It puts you on the same team.

While you're in the process of building rapport with the angry individual, avoid asking questions that begin with why. There is something about "why" that often puts people, particularly *upset* people, on the defensive. For example, "This isn't the way I like it, please take it back to the kitchen." "Why?" Now they are ticked off. "Because I asked you to. That's why!" Instead, when confronted with such a situation, try questions such as these:

- "Yes. How might I correct this situation for you?"
- "Yes. Can you please give me an example?"

- "Certainly. Could you please tell me what you think caused this?"
- "Of course. Would you mind helping me understand the full situation?"
- "Certainly. How did you come to this decision?"

To further develop rapport with an angry individual, you must master *feel, felt* and *found*. Here's how: "I understand how you *feel*, others have *felt* that way, but what they have *found* is, after purchasing...."

The first clause, "I understand how you *feel*" is saying "I am relating to you and I hear you. I am taking the time to listen to you." When you say, "Others have *felt* that way," you are saying, "You are not alone, it's okay to feel that way." When you say, "But what they have *found* is," you're saying that others have discovered a solution and that this solution can work for your customer, too. Remember, most people are followers, not leaders. They like the fact that someone else has tested the waters first and found them safe.

Step 4. Create the solution. When you feel the customer's anger has been diffused and you have established a good rapport, you can enter into a solution. First, find out what the customer wants! How tragic that most confrontations go on much longer than needed, merely because we never take the trouble to find out what the other side wants!

Try statements like:

- "How can we help correct this situation?"
- "What could we do to return ourselves to your good graces?"
- "What can I do to show you I am really sorry about this?"

Sometimes you can't actually provide the solution, but you can send the individual to someone who can: "I understand. To solve this, we need to have the advice of our service manager." If possible, quickly brief the manager in private (out of the customer's view so he or she doesn't feel "ganged-up" on).

This does not mean that you shouldn't do everything in your power to resolve the situation. Customers often are further aggravated when they are "passed off" to three or four different people, having to repeat their story each time. If you must bring in someone else, *stay with your customer,* so he or she doesn't feel abandoned. Offer to remain until the situation is resolved. If you feel that the customer is comfortable with the individual now in charge, then you can excuse yourself.

Step 5. Reconfirm your understanding. Once a satisfactory solution is found, it is important to reconfirm and review the situation and the specifics of the solution. Because of the emotional state the person may be in, it is likely that he or she may have heard or understood some of the particulars differently from how you meant to communicate them. Review carefully each step involved in the solution, even writing them out if appropriate.

Step 6. Follow through. If you handled this situation well, you have the opportunity to build a loyal connection with this person. But if you don't follow through, you may do serious damage and negate all your efforts to resolve the problem. To make sure you will follow through, take these steps:

- Send a written confirmation of the solution to which you have agreed.
- In your calendar write down each step and exactly when you are going to take it.
- Thank the customer, at each stage of the process, for his or her understanding.
- Add a touch of *uncommon* courtesy. Send a personalized and professional note, a box of candy or a small gift.

Keep in mind that customers remember most what you did when things went wrong. Be dynamic!

When a customer cannot be satisfied

Your goal is to make the other person happy. Unfortunately, and very rarely, you may not come to an understanding. If you can't get your dissatisfied customer to Step 4, and he or she acts abusive toward you, try a team-building statement: "Mr. Smith, let's work on a way we can fix this."

If that doesn't work, try addressing their hostile actions in a nondefensive way, attaching a team-building statement on the end. Try, "Mr. Smith, please don't yell at me. Let's work on a way to correct this situation."

If you just cannot establish rapport, it may be that you don't have the right "chemistry" with the individual. Rather than frustrate the customer further, it may be wisest to turn to a supervisor for assistance— just as you would if you didn't have the authority to sign off on a solution. Follow the same steps discussed previously in Step 4, making sure you don't make the individul feel he or she has been "dumped off" on someone else.

Managers and the Instinctive dynamic

As you grow in your abilities to use your natural Instinctive sonar, like dolphins do, you will find yourself using it in all aspects of your life—work *and* home.

Although everything we have discussed so far is appropriate to management as well as the front line businessperson, we have devoted this next section to situations that are unique to management. If you do not consider yourself management yet—don't skip this section! Someday you will need these skills.

Use your sonar to hire the right team

Dolphins stay in groups called "pods." In my very human opinion, they seem to view those around them as valued traveling companions. Organizations would not have devastating employee turnover if they took the time to look a bit more closely at the individuals they bring into their "pods," carefully selecting those they consider to be valued traveling companions.

When a company decides to bring a new employee on board, it expects this individual to make the company stronger, better and more profitable. Unfortunately, many employers are quickly disappointed.

So how do you keep this potentially positive situation from turning into a costly one? The following are several tips.

Ask employees for names of job candidates. Solicit names of potential candidates from current employees as well as professional associates, vendors and clients. These individuals will frequently know quality candidates. This can be especially helpful during times when it may be difficult to find a large quantity or a higher quality of candidates. Many times these referrals can make excellent employees because they may feel an obligation to go the extra mile because of their association with others involved in the company.

Design appealing advertisements. Determine what the most important characteristics are to the position and design an advertisement accordingly. In sales, for example, some of the most important traits may include a positive, outgoing, dynamic personality, professionalism, assertiveness, etc. These qualities generally are more important than industry experience and product knowledge, which can be acquired.

Create a qualifications and skills list. Have a list of qualifications and skills that you require and a list of other skills that would be beneficial but not necessarily required. If no proficiency standard is available, ask the candidates to rate their specific skill level on a scale of 1 to 10. Take the time to create a qualifications checklist before you hire someone. This will help you determine in what areas the applicants are strong and weak.

Keep the initial interview short. Limit your initial interview to no more than 15 minutes. Your first impression of the candidate is critical, especially in situations like sales, customer service and management where a great deal of interpersonal interaction is the mainstay of the position. Remember, your customers will be making the same quick judgment.

Prepare interview questions. Use open-ended questions to qualify your candidate. Don't ask, "Are you outgoing and enthusiastic?" A better question would be, "What two adjectives best describe you?" When you use open-ended questions, the candidate will volunteer more information. The candidate's choice of words, length of conversation, conversation style and body language will help you better assess the individual.

Your questions (see the following samples) should refer to specific elements that are important to the position. Don't be afraid to get the negatives out in the open. It's far better to hear them now rather than suffer the costly consequences later.

Sample hiring questions

- "What two adjectives best describe you?"
- "What is the ideal position for you in any company?"
- "What do you know about our company?"
- "Why would you like to work with us?"
- "What are your best professional skills?"
- "What was your biggest past failure in business?"
- "Describe a *great* day at the job of your dreams."
- "What are your personal interests and/or hobbies?"
- "What are your impressions of your previous work situation?"
- "What past successes (personal and professional) are you the most proud of?"
- "What are your goals for the next five years?"

Don't sell the position up front. Most interviewers hit a point of awkward silence during the interview. Some interviewers will start selling the position with something like, "Well, let me tell you about ABC Company..." The promotion of the company should be reserved for desired candidates near the end of the next interview. Instead, use the pause as an opportunity to watch how your candidate responds. See if the candidate attempts to connect with you during the silence.

Schedule a second interview. If a candidate is of interest to you, ask if he or she would like to be included in the second interview process. This will minimize calling back candidates you are interested in, only to find out that they are not interested in the position.

If the person isn't right for the position, kindly let him or her know immediately or tell him or her that you have others to interview. Inform him or her that all applicants will be contacted within 48 hours about a potential second interview.

The second interview is an opportunity for you to verify your initial impression, ask more questions and test the candidate's work ethic by seeing if he or she shows up on time.

If I am interviewing for a salesperson, I explain to the applicant that it is important for me to get to know someone's sales style and I ask the candidate to sell me something as simple as, let's say, a pencil. Excusing some nervousness, I watch for body language, customer involvement, price strategies and add-on capabilities. You would be amazed at how much information I receive from this one technique.

Hiring great candidates involves more skill than luck. The preparation dedicated up front will be made up quickly by brief initial interviews, saving you time and most importantly, by entrusting your customers to the best qualified candidate.

Employee discipline: how, when and why

If you are in management—or intend to be—you will find yourself in a position where it becomes necessary to discipline a member of your team. All leaders do. Be ready.

If you continually run into staff performance or behavioral issues, it might be wise to step back and assess your hiring practices, communication and managerial style. Go over the last one or two years and track your turnover ratio. Excessive turnover is very costly to any business. Evaluate the skill levels of your current employees with fun quizzes and by monitoring their work. You might find it necessary to change the way you interview job candidates, train staff or establish job expectations. Before you address an employee about poor performance or lament about the inferior quality of the work force these days, make sure you're providing the right training and management.

Recently I consulted with a retail sales manager who was having a few more employee challenges than he would have liked. He had one staff member who was occasionally rude to customers and another who became downright indignant over her disappointment in the schedule. Many of these situations occur because clear guidelines are not drawn. For example, do your employees know the consequences if they show up for work late? Do they know what is considered late? Is five minutes past the hour late? Fifteen minutes? Management must clearly define the rules and performance expectations, and communicate the consequences for breach of expectations and then follow up with the appropriate sequence of disciplinary action when called for.

Sequence for disciplinary action

Giving a verbal, documented warning is allowing your employee the opportunity to improve while demonstrating your resolve. If the behavior continues, document it again on a disciplinary form, this time checking off that this is a written warning rather than a verbal warning. When an employee makes the same mistake three times, you are probably dealing with an individual unwilling or unable to perform his or her job. In this situation, it is best for everyone that he or she move on.

It is very important to address issues such as employee tardiness immediately—even if they seem relatively minor. Many managers report that when one unacceptable behavior is tolerated or overlooked, other employees consciously or unconsciously act out. The next thing you know, you have a group of people giving you endless grief.

In addition to the value of having documentation of disciplinary action, there are other benefits to the writing-up process: First, the employee realizes that it is indeed a serious situation. And, perhaps even more important, it sends a strong message to others in the group. Even if the individual reports to his co-workers that you're a cruel and nasty person, the message that gets back to the group is "Boy, he stepped across the line and something bad happened, so I better follow the guidelines."

When an employee first crosses a line, take the responsibility upon yourself. Assume that you did not clarify your expectations clearly enough. You now have an opportunity to precisely clarify your expectations. Watch your vocabulary! Avoid words such as "try" and "I'd appreciate it if...." Replace them with, "Let me clarify the responsibilities of this position" and "I need this to happen...."

In the case of tardiness, what did you tell your employees starting time was? Many managers who expect their employees to start work at 10 a.m., tell them, "Starting time is 10 a.m." Instead say, "Your starting time is 10 a.m. That means you are to be on the floor and ready to serve our customers *by* 10 a.m. Allow yourself enough time to hang up your coat and finish your cup of coffee so you will be on the sales floor by 10 a.m. sharp." I would recommend a written memo that specifies attendance, start time and tardiness policies. Have your employees sign and return it. This increases accountability.

If an employee repeats an unacceptable behavior—say, he or she shows up late a second time in one month—this is your clue to be concerned. Clarify that he or she understood your instructions with a question such as, "Mike, when we talked about being on time before, what time do you recall we agreed that you would be on the sales floor ready to serve customers? Mike this will be a verbal warning that I am documenting on this sheet." (On most disciplinary forms, there is a place to check off for either a written or verbal warning as well as a place for the employee's comments and signature.)

Even verbal warnings should be documented on a disciplinary form. States such as New York require three documented written warnings on the same offense to discredit unemployment claims. There are some circumstances (theft, for example) where three warnings are not required. Consult your state unemployment agency for details and guidelines. Remember, while giving a verbal or written warning, address (not attack) the observable behavior rather than the person. This way you are allowing the employee to save face and improve without feeling embarrassed.

Terminating an employee

After an employee has exhibited unwillingness or inability to change, it is in the best interest of both the employer and the employee that termination of employment be pursued. If you are the employer, do not wait for the employee to leave—even though you may be tempted to do so in order to avoid the confrontation.

Firing can be the most challenging and stressful part of a manager's job duties. The following are suggestions and guidelines that should be followed only after all state and federal laws have been adhered to. They will assist you in reducing the stress of terminating.

- Stay calm. You need to be objective and use documentation as your foundation for the decision.

- Choose a neutral setting. Make sure that you have some privacy. Often, the human resources areas of businesses include a couple of small interview rooms. This might be an appropriate spot for your meeting.

- Transportation. Did the employee bring his or her own car? You don't want a person that was just terminated moping around the office while they are waiting for a bus. If the individual uses public transportation, wait until the end of the day to let him or her go.

- Final accommodations on insurance, vacation pay, final paychecks and outplacement services, if applicable, should be made ahead of time.

- The employee should not be surprised by the termination. Sufficient warning should have been given before terminating (excluding violations such as theft, safety or physical abuse).

- Be brief. The entire terminating session should take no longer than five minutes.

- Don't challenge the individual. Expect him or her to be upset, but don't respond to criticism or feel the need to engage in defensive dialogue.

- Briefly compliment the person on some characteristic and tie that into future success with another company.

- Don't negotiate. Be compassionate but firm. Your decision to terminate is based on documented failure to perform. Even though you may be tempted to "work something out," giving the employee "one more chance," you must remember that you've already given the employee opportunities to change and what you are doing is in the best interest of the company.

Quiz for the Instinctive Dynamic

1. Do you use your professional sonar, watching people around you like a dolphin—astutely observing their movements?
   ❑ Yes   ❑ No

2. Do you look for clues about a person from his or her office, business or home?
   ❑ Yes   ❑ No

3. Do you make an effort to repeat the customer's key concepts back to him or her during your conversations?
   ❑ Yes   ❑ No

4. Do you make an effort to plant questions in your customers' minds?
   ❑ Yes   ❑ No

5. Do you often say things such as, "That's interesting, tell me about it," to encourage a connection?
   ❑ Yes   ❑ No

6. Have you eliminated "How much do you want to spend?" and "What price range did you have in mind?" from your vocabulary?
   ❑ Yes   ❑ No

7. When appropriate, do you take notes while you are talking to a customer?
   ❑ Yes   ❑ No

8. Have you taken a survey of customer satisfaction in the past six months?
   ❑ Yes   ❑ No

9. Have you mastered the *feel, felt, found* system?
   ❑ Yes   ❑ No

10. Are you able to determine if someone is highly Determined, Instinctive, Vision-oriented or Enthusiastic?
    ❑ Yes   ❑ No

11. Do you observe people's handwriting to help you connect with them?
    ❑ Yes   ❑ No

12. Are you familiar with open-ended versus closed-ended questions?
    ❑ Yes   ❑ No

13. Do you ask mostly open-ended questions?
    ❑ Yes   ❑ No

14. Do you make a conscious effort to make those around you feel important, appreciated, respected, remembered, understood and secure?
    ❑ Yes   ❑ No

15. Do you adjust your approach to customers or co-workers based on their body language, personality, background, etc.?
    ❑ Yes   ❑ No

16. Are you training yourself to recognize verbal or nonverbal signs of commitment from your customers (or your employees)?
    ❑ Yes   ❑ No

17. Do you put your commitments from customers in writing as soon as you have them?
    ❑ Yes   ❑ No

18. Are you able to listen to emotional customers, rather than react to them?
    ❑ Yes   ❑ No

19. Do you position yourself just within the customer's personal zone?
    ❑ Yes   ❑ No

20. Have you eliminated the word "why" from your vocabulary when dealing with angry customers?
    ❑ Yes   ❑ No

If you answered 18 to 20 yes's, you exhibit a high degree of dolphin-like Instinct and will increase your success rapidly.

If you answered 13 to 17 yes's, beware—sharks are in the water with you.

If you answered 10 to 12 yes's, you are wounded and sharks are moving in.

If you answered nine or less yes's, *get out of the water*—you are about to be eaten alive!

Checklist for the Instinctive Dynamic

• When trying to connect with a customer, client or co-worker, watch the direction of the person's body. If turned away from you, he or she may not be attentive or may want to get away.

• Step closer to people to be just inside their personal zone.

• Match the pace of the people you are trying to connect with, then slowly build to a faster pace.

• When you see signs of boredom, such as tapping feet, wandering eyes and watch-checking, grab the person's attention by handing him or her something, getting him or her moving and speeding up a little bit.

• When you see signs of confusion, accept responsibility and apologize for being unclear.

• Spend two hours a week watching people in different situations and places.

• While giving a verbal or written warning, address (not attack) the observable behavior, not the person.

• Ask open-ended questions—help the customer to give you the information you need.

• Use a Career Profile Assessment to help identify the ideal candidate when hiring.

• Survey your customers—internal *and* external—to stay in touch with their needs, and be sure to reward them for their time.

• Maintain appropriate eye contact with your customers, and don't forget to smile.

• Remember: A great communicator is one who listens and watches carefully, then asks the appropriate questions, then listens again.

• Learn to read commitment signals—verbal or nonverbal expressions that suggest readiness by the customer—and be ready to act on them.

- Learn handwriting analysis as another means of recognizing silent signals from customers, employees or co-workers.

- Plan to resolve issues—even if the customer isn't planning to—and you most likely will resolve them.

- Always use positive body language—open hand gestures, smiling, etc.

- When dealing with angry customers, avoid "why" questions.

- Be sure to address employee problems promptly—even if they seem relatively minor.

- Learn to recognize the personality types—Determined, Instinctive, Visionary or Enthusiastic—in order to better connect with them.

In conclusion about Instinct

This section, focusing on the Instinctive Dynamic, offers insights, tips and techniques to help you tune in, interpret and understand those around you. Using dolphin-like "sonar" will give you exceptional connection capabilities, both personally and professionally. In business, this power this will give you a strong competitive advantage.

The techniques described in this section have amazed countless people who have taken the time and energy to tune in to their customers, co-workers, clients and other business associates. You have the capability to unleash your professional and personal sonar. To do so, you need to become an astute observer, acute listener and a perceptive professional.

Dynamic Three: Vision

In this dynamic you will learn:

- How goal-setting will increase your productivity and income.
- How to take mental and physical possession of your vision.
- How to use incentives and sales contests to increase business.

So far, we've learned the importance of Determination and Instinct in our professional and personal success. Vision is the next important component. Without it, we don't have a target for our Determination and Instinct. Our Vision provides our destination. It is our mind's ability to imagine what is possible.

If you don't know where you're going, any road will take you there."

—Unknown

Determination and Instincts must be combined with your relentless reach for a dream, a Vision—the place you are going and the things you want. All the Determination, Enthusiasm and Instinctiveness in the world does you no good if you don't have a Vision to guide the dynamics.

"The world turns aside to let any man pass who knows where he is going."

—David Starr Jordan, U.S. biologist,
first president of Stanford University

Stationing: a technique for clearer Vision

Dolphins, like humans, do better by focusing their energies and talents prior to performing a challenging task. Dolphin trainers "station" the dolphins before they start a training behavior. This is achieved by a hand gesture that lets the dolphins know, "Time to get focused—something great is going to happen here and you're going to do it." The trainer simply holds a hand in an upward pointing gesture, establishes eye contact and gives the behavior command.

In an environment such as a sea park, or even in a quiet place such as the Dolphin Research Center, there are many distractions for dolphins. There are people gawking, other dolphins and hungry seagulls trying to steal their fish.

Sounds just like business. Managers and owners have budgets to design and assess, advertising to place and monitor, employees to train and motivate. Salespeople have customers to visit, cold calls to make and inventory to fill. The business world is filled with an ocean of distractions.

By focusing on your Vision—or "stationing"—you will be able to drown out the distractions and hit your professional and personal targets. Stationing, before you begin any task, will increase your effectiveness, even if your goal is simply to have fun.

Vision—station—DIVE!

If you want to be a top salesperson or own a highly successful and profitable business—or achieve anything exceptional—you must learn to set goals! If you are a leader in your organization, please understand that you cannot cultivate goal-setters until *you* are a goal-setter!

Goals are a charting device. They let you know where you are going and how you are doing. However, poorly defined goals are not going to result in success. The power of realizing and obtaining your goals is in direct proportion to your visualization of your goals. *Goals must be written down.* In this section, you will learn how to master the skill of goal-setting for the purpose of achieving your long-term Vision. In the next few pages I will show you how goal-setting has produced incredible things for me and for my clients—and how goal-setting can do the same for you.

You should have goals for the big things in your life—as well as your day-to-day workings. Goals will help make each day, month and year more productive and successful for you. Goals tell you how close or far you are to your long-term Vision.

The human mind is like a missile. Give your mind a target, work at it and you will hit it. With no goal, your mind will use its valuable energy searching and searching, fatally falling short of its target.

Let me explain the difference between Vision and goals. Vision is the overall picture of where you want to be in, let's say, 10 or 20 years, with all of the specifics. Goals are the measurable achievements along the way.

If you were like me as a child, you were probably told to pay attention and stop daydreaming. I hate to contradict my elders, but it is critical to daydream, no matter how old you are. Where do you want to be in 10 years? In 20 years? What style of home do you want to live in? Who do you want around you? Your mind will help you get there if you take the time to imagine it.

Shaping your success

"Shaping" is the positive reinforcement of a favorable behavior. Shaping is a critical step in achieving success and is also used in dolphin training. Dolphins generally don't do the type of high dives you see in a sea park on their own. Generally, the dolphin trainer breaks the ultimate desired behavior down into smaller, more achievable steps. The trainer catches the dolphin doing a small part of a high dive. It may be the dolphin simply tucking its head down as it surfaces for air or the dolphin may jump out of the water a little bit. When the dolphin does this, the trainer rewards the dolphin with a fish. The trainer is "shaping" the dolphin's behavior.

I don't think I can get you too excited with juicy, raw fish. So you need to figure out what will motivate you to perform substantial goals along your journey toward your Vision. These are your rewards. Anytime you set a goal for yourself, you must set a reward that will help motivate you to work as hard as you need to accomplish the goal. This shaping will make hitting your own target more exciting and probable. Remember, your goals should be challenging, so set yourself an exciting reward. We will discuss specific guidelines on rewards in a few pages.

"Life has a meaning only if one barters it day by day for something other than itself."

—Antoine de Saint-Exupéry,
French writer and aviator

Visualization

Dolphins also seem to use mental visualization to hit their targets. I was amazed to observe dolphins performing a high dive. The dolphins were given a target to touch with their nose. Then the dolphins stuck their head out of the water, visualizing their target. Once the dolphins visualized the target, they went underwater, gathering sufficient momentum, and hit their target. To prove that dolphins plan their momentum, the dolphin trainers moved the target after the dolphin had left the water. The dolphins pursued what they visualized—staying totally focused.

In addition, during training exercises or migration, dolphins often travel in dangerous waters, thriving by staying focused on their target. When faced with obstacles, they outmaneuver, outswim and, when necessary, take predators such as sharks head on. Despite the challenges they face, they ultimately stay on course whether that course is life-sustaining or enjoyment-oriented.

When you set high, yet realistic, goals and visualize yourself meeting those standards, this alone will greatly improve the chances of hitting your targets. I was recently asked to present a written assessment of a company's retail sales force. In observing the team in action, I noticed that prior to beginning their shift on the sales floor, the top performers were filling out what seemed to be an inordinate number of sales invoices with their name and sales number. I was impressed that these men and women usually met or exceeded their allotment of invoices. It was their way of setting goals for themselves at the beginning of the day.

The power of posting

The powerful strategy of writing down your Visions will greatly increase your chances for obtaining them. If you don't write them down you are only dreaming. The process of writing down your thoughts can change dreams into reality. When you write down your dreams *and, better yet, post them in a highly visible place,* you are helping your mind find and clear a path. Once you have determined what you want, you can figure out what you have to do to get there.

This strategy will also help you accomplish minor tasks, the steps along the way that bring you closer to your Visions. I even find that writing down tasks helps me accomplish such simple things as cleaning the house more quickly.

Goal charts

Before you begin, you may need to give some thought to what your Vision is. Think about where you want to be in the future. Now let's be specific. Let your mind wander. Where do you want to be in five years, in 10 and 20 years? What position do you want to hold? Where do you want to live? Who do you want in your life? What financial status do you want to obtain? If you plan to have children, will they go to college? If so, where? What kinds of vehicles do you want to own (cars, planes, boats)? What color will they be? The more specific you allow yourself to be, the more you will be able to unleash your mind, the more you will be able to plan and the more successful you will be in achieving your Vision.

I recommend that you begin increasing your Visionary skills with monthly goals. It's great practice for great things. For example, if a major goal of yours is to become the top salesperson in your company, then write it down.

Now determine your time frame. So *when* will you be the top salesperson for your company—which month? Now, what can you accomplish this month to work toward that Vision?

For those of you who want to put this into a database, fine—if you work in front of a computer all day and you can program the computer to run your goals in front of you at any time. *But*, if you don't have your face buried in your computer screen all the time, you must also put this on a chart, on the wall, and in other strategic, highly visible places such as on the dashboard of your car, on your bathroom mirror, on the refrigerator, or wherever it is that you spend time.

Posted goals are a powerful reminder to yourself and others of how you are doing. Some people have said they don't want to "clutter up" the wall of their tastefully decorated office with a goal chart. That goal chart can and will pay for that wall and building and the next office complex you buy when this procedure is followed properly. Posting goals and progress is also beneficial in a sales environment because it can assist in healthy competitiveness.

Here is a chart that I use to track and encourage my success. I'm confident it will help you also.

A	B	C	D	E
Today's date:	*Vision:*	*Tasks needed to accomplish:*	*The date I will accomplish this:*	*I will reward myself by:*
4/1/96	Be the top salesperson in my company.			
4/1/96	Own a 20-plus-foot boat.			
4/1/96	Have $100,000 in the bank.			

How does it work? Let's talk about becoming the top salesperson in your company. Write down what activities or tasks it will take to make that happen. Perhaps start with the number of units you have to sell to get there.

Now, the hard part, write down areas in which you need to improve. You probably will need to have another person assess you in order to provide more objectivity to the process. Areas that may require attention and improvement might include: better, more dynamic greetings; maintaining friendly control; using assumptive gestures and vocabulary that assist you in obtaining sales. Now, decide how long you will give yourself to reach this top level. Write that date down. Notice that this category is not titled "When it would be nice," or "When I might want to accomplish it."

The power of assumptive vocabulary is at work here also. By using words like "will" instead of "might," you are helping your mind take possession of your goals. Using words like "your" instead of "the" will help your customers imagine taking mental possession, therefore increasing your chances of obtaining a sale. As powerful as assumptive vocabulary is at obtaining sales, it is just as powerful at convincing yourself you will achieve your goals.

Finally, decide on your reward once you have achieved your goal— better yet, the reward your *family* and you will receive when you achieve your goal! Try to make your reward in line with the goal you've achieved. I try not to spend more than 10 percent of my achievement on my reward. If you are like me, you want nice things. This guideline and my husband, Joe, help to keep me out of trouble. Don't, for example, reward yourself with a new VCR if your goal is to clean the house. A more appropriate reward may be a hot bath, a long walk or ice cream with the kids (out of the clean house). Some of the best rewards are free, such as time with your family or friends.

My goal was to write and have this book accepted by a progressive publisher by my 30th birthday. The entire project was a major challenge. It was a sincere combination of Determination (which helped me through the minor and major disturbances), Instinct (allowing me to make decisions about whom to associate with and which paths to take), Vision (seeing myself as a published author) and the Enthusiasm to help me along the way. All goals should be realistic but challenging.

Let's look at another goal-setting scenario—a simple goal such as cleaning the house. (See page 142.) Okay, now what tasks go into accomplishing this goal? Now, decide how long each one of these activities or tasks will take. What will your reward be when you complete cleaning the house? Eliminate distractions and get started!

Cleaning the house

A Date/time to be completed	B Tasks to be done	C Reward
2:45 3:15 3:30 3:45 4:00	Clean the bathrooms Vacuum Clean the windows Wash the floors Polish the furniture	

Bar charts

I use a bar chart to stay on track at achieving my sales goals. But such a tool will help you whether you are a salesperson, manager or owner. A bar chart records your progress along the way. Monthly goals are an excellent way to get you on the path of attaining your long-term Visions.

```
Feb. 28———$100,000
Feb. 27———
Feb. 26———
Feb. 25———
Feb. 24———
Feb. 23———
Feb. 22———
Feb. 21———
Feb. 20———
Feb. 19———
Feb. 18———
Feb. 17———
Feb. 16———
Feb. 15———
Feb. 14———
Feb. 13———
Feb. 12———
Feb. 11———
Feb. 10———
Feb. 9———
Feb. 8———
Feb. 7———
Feb. 6———
Feb. 5———$8,225
Feb. 4———$8,000
Feb. 3———$5,100
Feb. 2———$4,250
Feb. 1———$2,000
```

To choose a monthly goal, I figure out where I want to end up at the end of the month. I make this decision based on a challenging yet realistic goal that is in proportion to my long-term Vision. I really, really must want it. Let's say I decide my goal will be $100,000 worth of sales for the month of February. Now I get out a piece of poster board and draw a bar chart (shown here). Then I draw in my projected success. I keep the chart in a highly visible place, yet out of the view of external customers.

As I obtain a sale, I color in the appropriate amount, adding as I go along. On the left side of this chart I write the date. This way I can track my progress in comparison to the time remaining.

Activity charts

Next is an activity chart (shown below), which represents the tasks that have been proven successful in acquiring clients. This will vary slightly from business to business. I have customized this list for many clients. I will explain each column, and how I use them.

Goal for this month—$100,000 in new sales

The first row of letters, from left to right, are not on the chart in my office. They are here merely to help me explain this chart to you.

A	B	C	D	E	F	G	H	I	J	K
# of needed sales	Date	Cust. name	Phone #	Appt.	Thank-you note	Sold	Follow-up call	Referrals	Second appt.	Amount
1.										
2.										
3.										
4.										
5.										

Column A: number of needed sales. I need to know what my average sale and my current closing ratio is to properly assess how many potential customers I have to contact. For simplicity's sake, let's say I have a $10,000 average sale (not bad if you're selling toothbrushes, not good if you're selling Rolls Royces!). If my closing ratio is 50 percent, then I would need to find 20 potential customers. The trouble is, if I count on 10 closings, I will fall short of my goal because of normal postponements or cancellations. So I count on the number I need *plus* 20 percent—in this case 12 (see row A). Always overshoot your goal. It is far more rewarding to say you sold *more than* $100,000, rather than *almost* $100,000.

I now know that I need 12 clients a month at an average sale of $10,000 to hit my goal. This is much easier to understand and more palatable than just saying I need $120,000 in sales. Divide the amount of sales by the number of working days in the month, and I know my daily goal.

Now I go to my day planner (as well as notes on bathroom mirror, dashboard, etc.) and write down my daily goals. If I ever fall short of obtaining my daily goal, I roll over the deficit to the next day's goal. If it is a huge number, I spread the deficit evenly over my daily activities for the month.

Columns B, C, D: date, customer name and phone number. Fill in the date of your initial appointment with each customer. This helps you plan your work for the month and see where you might have "holes," opportunities to schedule other productive activity.

By following this system, you're more likely to have a constant stream of activity. Then fill in Columns C and D, your customer's name and phone number. I make the phone number prominent, so it encourages me to call. This allows me to follow up with the customer often, which is a key to strong connections and beating your competition.

Column E: appointment. I put a check here once the appointment actually holds. This system acts as a reminder to call back if, by chance, the customer needed to postpone or reschedule.

Column F: thank-you's. This column reminds me to send a thank-you note. I put the date that I sent the note here. I recommend that you send thank-you notes whether or not you obtain the sale that day.

A thank-you note shows appreciation, respect and extra effort. I recommend a handwritten, personalized message such as:

Dear Bob:

It was great meeting with you. I am confident that you are going to enjoy your gorgeous new office furniture. I look forward to working with you and your company and will follow up with you shortly.

Dynamically,

Laura

Laura

Column G: Sold! Enter the date on which you obtained the sale so you can track how long it takes each person or yourself on average to obtain a sale. You may notice patterns—one person may have a much higher percentage of closes the same day, compared to another who takes much longer. This is valuable information for a sales manager or owner. You now have begun to isolate specific areas for further staff development. If you have a salesperson, for example, who takes much longer to close than your other salespeople, you can provide that person with the needed training.

Be careful, however. Don't let *your* mind or *other* people's words play tricks on you. I have worked with numerous businesses who swore that their product and service required more than one call. I was able to show them, hands on, that was simply not the case. Some businesses require more than one call but a majority do not.

Column H: follow-up phone calls. If you didn't get the order while you were with your customer, the better your follow-up skills, the higher the chances are for an eventual sale. This column is also valuable for letting salespeople know that you expect follow-up. This chart will reveal people's reluctance to call customers back. When you isolate a weakness, you should provide the employees with training or coaching to help them improve their skills.

As we discussed previously in Determination, it is critical for your customers to feel that they are worth the extra effort. You need to demonstrate that you are the type of person who is not only willing, but eager to provide more than expected. Many people are reluctant to call their customers back. They feel they will be bothering them. If you have connected with your customers during your time with them and exemplified the traits of a dynamic professional, they will not be put off—they will be impressed. This is another strategic and powerful edge over the competition. I recommend follow-up within 24 to 48 hours after your first encounter.

There should be more than enough columns for follow-up conversations on the board. High-end retail, for example, probably requires no more than three, but large, business-to-business enterprises can require as many as eight. How often do you follow up? Until you obtain the sale!

Column I: referrals. In this column, I put an X for each referral I receive.

Column J: second appointments. For some businesses, more than one contact with a customer or client is often required. In this case, I'd add columns for second and third contacts with customers.

Column K: amount of sale. Write down the amount of the proposed sale, whether or not you obtained it. This will give you, the management and/or owner, an idea of what merchandise or services you are suggesting to your customers.

Monitor your progress

As you formalize the goal-setting process, write down scheduled check dates in your planner to monitor your progress along the way. If you find yourself below the appropriate measurement at a scheduled time, readjust the required activity. For example, let's say your goal was to sell 100 widgets, and on the 15th of the month you open your planner and it tells you to check your goal. You do and discover you have only sold 40 widgets. Now you can fold the difference of where you should be and where you are, by rolling that over into your remaining time.

Star boards

Like all parents, I want my children to accomplish great things, to be able to make a splash in their futures, conquering any sharks along the way. I use star boards to help encourage and reward my children for accomplishing extraordinary things.

When my older son Craig wants something extra-special and there is no holiday in sight, we increase the value of the item and develop Craig's work ethic by having him "earn" it. Joe and I decide on the activity needed to receive the reward. Then we get a piece of poster board and star stickers and paste a picture or symbol of the reward on the star board. When Craig accomplishes one of the necessary tasks, he gets a star. Generally, he needs only 10 or 20 stars to get his reward. Yes, Craig receives presents "just because." But this star board system helps him understand that he is in control of what he accomplishes and receives. And Derek, now just 3, is working on his first star board.

Mental possession

If your goal is to become a manager in your company, then imagine what your desk will look like. If you want to become successful enough to afford new carpet for your home or office then figure out what color, texture and how the carpet will feel. If your Vision is a new office building, help your mind get you there by telling it where your building will be located and what the decor will look like. In the case of the carpet and the office building, I would also recommend you go shopping for them.

Approximately five years ago, I was leafing through a home magazine, daydreaming, and found a picture of a breathtaking home. I cut out the picture and showed it to Joe. By the look on his face, I could tell he wanted to say, "Yeah right, and exactly how are we going to afford that?" At the time, we owned a comfortable two-family home. Over the next year I continued clipping out pictures of just what I wanted my dream home to look like. I cut them out and hung them up on my refrigerator. Four bedrooms a must. Bathrooms? At least three! An open kitchen overlooking the family room. Oh yeah, and at least 3,000 square feet.

When Joe and I went house hunting, we were still only looking at modest homes. We were about to leave yet another modest home that we were not thrilled with when the realtor asked if we would look at another home out of the city. I was reluctant because of the location. It was 60 minutes south of a major city, but Joe wanted to look. So off we went to the country.

On the long drive there, I was trying to keep the boys occupied when, finally, we turned into a driveway. I looked up. My dream house! Joe and I looked at each other in disbelief. A large home, four bedrooms, four bathrooms, the kitchen overlooking the family room with a cathedral ceiling! Joe's first words: "Laura, I can't believe it. It's like all of the pictures." We all live there today—me, Joe, the boys and the dogs. Don't ask me how to explain this one. I don't question the results I receive from goal-setting anymore, I just keep going.

Another way I take mental possession in my professional life is by envisioning a strong connection with my customers. When I am on a sales call, I carry an agreement (as opposed to calling it a threatening and intimidating word like contract)! I don't go in just to gather information. My Vision is to connect this person with me, my product, service or the idea.

Put up something that reminds you every day, several times a day, of your goal—a picture, a figure, the words. And make sure you put it in a very visible spot.

Combining mental and physical possession

Taking mental possession of your goals means visualization, dreaming the dream, feeling it and tasting it, even though you don't own it yet. Taking physical possession of a dream means finding ways to feel it and touch it. Combining mental and physical possession is a great way to make your goals and Visions come true.

Many years ago, when I began selling Mary Kay cosmetics, I was told I could earn a company car. It took only three consecutive months of especially high achievement. Only a small percentage of Mary Kay people ever hit this mark. I was Determined and took mental possession of the car by getting picture postcards of the car from my director and pasting them on my refrigerator, on my date book, on the dash of my soon-to-be-replaced car and my bathroom mirror.

These images soon became a conversation topic. When people asked me why I had a picture of a car posted all over, I responded with "That's my new car."

Those three months were long and tough. Many people along the way (including Joe) thought that it couldn't be done. My drive began to sag. My director, Barb, gave me the idea to take physical possession of the car. She suggested I go to an Oldsmobile dealer and ask for a test drive. It did the trick! (You can be sure I hardly gloated, smirked or turned a smug expression to Joe when I picked him up for lunch weeks later, handed him the keys, and asked him if he wanted to drive my new car.)

Our closest major football team is the Buffalo Bills. You football fans may realize that the Buffalo Bills have the distinct record of being the only team in NFL history to have gone to the Super Bowl four consecutive times...losing each time. Well, at least they have some claim to fame.

Before the fourth trip to the Super Bowl the coach of the Buffalo Bills, Marv Levy, was asked to do the customary photo shoot with the Vince Lombardi trophy, which is awarded to the winner of the Super Bowl. It has been reported that Marv Levy didn't like taking pictures with or even touching the trophy. It is said that he felt it was bad luck.

However, after the Bills' failure at three Super Bowls, he evidently changed his mind.

During the photo session, Joe and I watched as he appeared uncomfortable. In contrast, his opponent Jimmy Johnson (former coach of the Dallas Cowboys) grabbed the trophy, embracing it enthusiastically, and pretended to walk away as if he had already won it. Is it coincidental that Jimmy was anxious to grab what appeared and ended up to be his trophy? I think not.

As we watched all this, I predicted to Joe that the Bills wouldn't win. I feel the Bills' struggles were *not* because they lacked talent, but because they feared success. I didn't believe the Bills' coaching staff or team saw themselves as Super Bowl winners.

When you take possession of something, even temporarily, your mind can more easily imagine keeping it. Then with Determination, you can map out how to permanently obtain it. The power of possession may be hard to understand but it is also hard to deny. The power of possession is a key in realizing your Vision, whatever type of business you are in. Embrace and master mental and physical possession.

Help customers envision themselves sold!

When you are showing a customer a product, who is the best person to hold it? You? No. *You* are not going to be the one taking it home. So hand it to your customer. Over and over again, this technique has been proven to increase customer satisfaction and sales. While this technique sometimes will take more time, the result will be more sales.

Positive internal talk: the law of expectation

- People who envision themselves as lucky are luckier.
- People who feel they are accident-prone are.
- People who feel successful are more successful.

Once you have a goal, you will need to utilize your mental and physical Determination to achieve it. The mental energy you must invest is just as demanding as the physical effort. You've probably felt physically exhausted, but have you ever felt mentally exhausted? I have many times and it's not a bad thing. Often in my professional growth, people have questioned and snickered at my goals, as they will at some of yours. Instead of allowing their shortsightedness to undermine your growth and success, learn to listen to the only person who can ultimately control your destiny—you!

Any time someone questions me, gives a skeptical look, or says something like, "What makes you think you can do that?" I tell myself and often them, "I don't think I can, I *know* I can." The resolve that comes from this mental reinforcement of my commitment is another key in the positive end results. If you expect to attain your goal, you will!

No matter how difficult things are, no matter how challenging things are, don't give up. Always speak to yourself and others as if you will accomplish and obtain your goals and vision.

Weak	**Assumptive**
Maybe.	*Yes,* I can.
I'll *try.*	I *will* do this.
If I do this...	*When* I do this...
I am *trying* to earn this car.	I am *going* to earn this car.
This is a picture of *the* house I'm working toward.	This is a picture of *my* house.

Help your team with profitable contests and incentives

One major challenge for most salespeople is making sure they have goals to aim for. Contests and incentives are great ways of encouraging yourself and your team to meet and exceed goals. Certainly my Determination, Instinct, Vision and Enthusiasm made me rise to the top and stay there. (Hunger and fear were great incentives for me in my early days, too!) Yet there were some smart things my employers did that encouraged me to work even harder: contests and incentives.

The restaurant I worked in when I was 16 had a holiday contest for staff—who could sell the most ice-cream dessert rolls. Most of the other waitresses found the thought of the contest annoying, but sales has always been my forte. I began suggesting, "A slice of our wonderful holiday ice-cream roll for dessert?" to all of my customers. When I checked back with them to see how they liked it, they said they loved it and I would quickly suggest a roll for the road. Or, "It is very convenient to have a festive dessert on hand at home!" Once I got "rolling," I sold more than 150 rolls in less than three weeks. I won the contest, earned the commission, and loved the excitement and the sense of accomplishment.

When I applied for work at my first "real" sales job, the owner told me the compensation was minimum wage plus an escalating commission rate of 1, 2 and 3 percent. Something felt very, very wrong with the thought of working for minimum wage, even though my commissions would surpass the base rate. So I, at the age of 16, offered to work for straight commission. The owner was pleasantly surprised and offered me an escalating rate of 7, 8 and 9 percent commission. We both did very well.

Almost every month there was a sales contest. At first the contests could only have one winner. The other employees became frustrated and sometimes didn't even try to compete because I always won. Then the owner designed contests that each and every one of his salespeople could win. Great idea! If you offer a contest that has only one or two winners, the others lose motivation knowing the superstars in the company will probably win it anyway.

Sales contests are different from quotas. Quotas (I prefer to call them standards) are a way of saying, "This is the requirement of the position—or else!" Sales contests are positive, not negative. Sales contests do, however, allow you to measure performance. They can tell you when an employee is marginal, in a risk situation or a top performer. Sales contests should supersede the sales standards. You will find the combination very powerful and profitable.

The challenge most salespeople have is in making sure they have goals to aim for. Some sales departments (for reasons I understand but do not agree with) do not have ongoing sales contests. If you are a salesperson and find yourself in this sort of company, I strongly recommend that you set your own goals religiously and then take the reward you've earned, remembering to set your next goal.

The benefits of sales contests

If set up properly, sales contests should not "cost" the company a dime. In fact, they will make you money.

Some of the benefits of sales contests are:

- They'll help move not-so-popular merchandise.
- They'll increase employee morale.
- They'll keep employees motivated by promoting healthy competition.

One of my first and favorite bosses, Ken, set up an excellent sales contest. Ken owned a waterbed store. Ken always encouraged us to sell care packs, supplies of materials and tools to take care of a waterbed. A partial, mini-version of this came with the waterbed, so many salespeople viewed the larger care pack as frivolous. Ken set up a contest that went like this: When we sold 20 care packs a month, we received $100. What did we get when you sold 19? Nothing. As with other good contests, everyone could win. Know-it-all that I was, I asked if we got $200 if we sold 40 care packs. He smiled and said that he hadn't sold 40 care packs in the last year, but, sure, for every 20 you sell, you will receive $100. I liked that contest. I made $300 dollars.

Even though Ken paid out $600, this contest was quite profitable for the company. The care packs sold for $30. Let's say the cost was $10. The bonus was $5. For every 20 he sold, he made $300. In other words, based on selling 120 care packs, his profit was $1,800 after paying out the bonuses. A win for the customer, a win for the salesperson and a win for Ken.

I once was helping a client train his salespeople. I explained to my client, Mark Mekota, that salespeople needed targets and rewards. Mark is one of the most financially astute people I know. He has an accounting background and when he says something works financially, it does. He modified a sales contest into the following five-tiered contest that rewards his salespeople for going beyond their comfort levels.

Each salesperson receives $50 for doing each of the following:

- Reaching his or her monthly sales goal.
- Reaching an average sale of more than $1,000. (Within just a few short months after training and this bonus structure, the average sale was over $1,200. Make sure to let your salespeople know up front in a pleasant but matter-of-fact way that this goal will vary month to month.)
- Achieving the established closing ratio. (Again, he set this just above where they currently are and moves it up slowly.)
- Attaining an appropriate number of referrals.
- The final component varied from contest to contest. (As with any goal, make it challenging, realistic, qualitative and measurable.)

All of these bonuses totals $250. If the person achieved all of the criteria, Mark doubled it to $500. Great incentive! When you customize a bonus structure for your company, you should have it set up in such a way that will be quite rewarding to the company as well. If an employee did each of these things, Mark was thrilled to reward the $500.

Shortsighted owners or managers tend to think, "I don't want to pay my people $500. Why should I pay them for doing their job?" Progressive owners or managers, however, know that by setting up a contest properly, you will be encouraging and motivating your salespeople to go beyond the call of duty and increasing profits for the company.

Designing just the right sales contest can be challenging—I know, I spend a great deal of my time designing them for my clients! Should you decide to create your own sales contest, keep these tips in mind:

- Make the goals challenging, yet achievable.
- Make the rewards something your team is interested in, not just you.
- Communicate all the goals and rules for the contest to all levels of your team.

Your Vision will take Determination

You must have a passionate desire to achieve your Vision. If you don't *really* want your Vision, you won't pay the price for accomplishing it.

As a trainer, I have the opportunity to give advice. Then clients and their employees go out and implement the strategies. Now, the neat part is when I talk to them six months later and they say, "Wow! All this great stuff happened...all because of you!"

During one of my goal-setting and time management seminars, a woman told the whole group that she had been to last year's course. I smiled and said, "This can go one of two ways. Either you really liked what you heard the first time or you have some unanswered questions." Happily, she told us that she had accomplished every one of the short-term goals she had set at that seminar and was ready for more! Her accomplishments from the last seminar were becoming a manager in her department, becoming engaged to her boyfriend, buying a home and finishing two college courses!

I was proud. Let me point out, while she gave me credit for directing her to achieve her goals, it was her own Vision—combined with Determination, Instinct and Enthusiasm—that really got her there. However, I will happily take all the credit the next time you see me if you follow these steps and reach your goals!

1. **Keep setting new goals.** Once they have accomplished a goal, most people get so excited they forget to set their next month's goal. Goal-setting is an ongoing process. As you achieve one set of goals, you should be developing new goals.

2. **Work with others to achieve your goals.** Goals may be achieved despite people, through people or with the help of people. It's easier with the help of people. Most people, when they commit to work at it, accomplish their goals. However, goals are small steps, significant strides or leaps to reaching a Vision.

3. Overcome your mental blocks and prejudices. Be careful. There are all sorts of things that can interfere with your positive imaging: fear of rejection, fear of failure, fear of success, lack of faith in your product or yourself or pre-conceptions based on past experience. These are all lethal in business.

When you walk into a meeting with thoughts like, "I don't know why I'm wasting my time, this guy is never going to buy anyway," you have effectively struck out before you ever stepped into the batter's box.

I was training a group of managers and sales personnel in improving their visualization techniques. During a break, one of the salespeople started talking to me about some successes he had in using mental visualization. Then he launched into a story about an incident where the technique proved ineffective.

"I was going on a sales call to someone's home, when I noticed a 'Proud to be Scottish' bumper sticker on the customer's car," the salesman recounted. "At that moment, I could feel myself becoming negative and skeptical about the sale."

This salesman went on to relate that he perceived those of Scottish descent to be "extremely cheap." At this point, he was using the bumper sticker as an excuse to fail. Not surprisingly, he did not make the sale to that customer—not because of that gentleman's heritage but because of his own mental blocks and prejudices.

I only wish I could have videotaped that particular sales call. I am confident I could have demonstrated that this salesperson was conveying negative verbal and nonverbal messages that ensured he would end up not making the sale.

"All our dreams can come true—if we have the courage to pursue them."
—Walt Disney

In another example, I was accompanying a salesperson on his calls. After the first two calls, during neither of which he'd sold his company's in-home product, I started making some suggestions. He responded with, "Okay, hotshot, I'd like you to do the next call." We arrived at a home that was well below the standard of most of the homes he worked with. We couldn't even go in the home because it was too messy. Instead, we sat outside on patio chairs that had holes so huge that I almost fell through. The table was rusted through, so I couldn't put my materials on it for fear it would collapse.

Early on I happened to glance at my friend who looked at me with triumph at my anticipated defeat. But instead of qualifying this couple as "lower-economic," I made a connection with my customers. In this case it was easy—they were very nice people. I simply customized my presentation to their desires. The result? A $2,200 sale. Check in hand. When you are aware of a predisposition to expect failure rather than success, you can evaluate the cause of this negativity, recognize it as irrational and alter your negative visualization to one that is positive.

Never, never prejudge your customers. Instead follow the techniques in this book to connect with your customers and you will be just as impressed with the results as my friend was.

What great minds have said about setting goals

"People with goals succeed because they know where they're going."
—Earl Nightingale, motivational radio talk show host, writer and speaker

"The world has the habit of making room for the man whose work and actions show that he knows where he is going."
—Napoleon Hill, author, *Think & Grow Rich*

The Dolphin Dynamic

"In the long run, men hit only what they aim at. Therefore...they had better aim at something high."
—Henry David Thoreau, U.S. philosopher, author and naturalist

"I have always thought that one man of tolerable abilities may work great changes, and accomplish great affairs among mankind, if he first forms a good plan, and, cutting off all amusements or other employments that would divert his attention, makes the execution of that same plan his sole study and business."
—Benjamin Franklin, U.S. statesman and writer

"The aims of life are the best defense against death."
—Primo Levi, Italian author, *The Drowned and the Saved*

"Without a purpose, nothing should be done."
—Marcus Aurelius, Roman emperor and Stoic philosopher

"Human happiness and moral duty are inseparately connected."
—George Washington

"Our plans miscarry because they have no aim. When a man does not know what harbor he is making for, no wind is the right wind."
—Seneca, Roman writer, philosopher and statesman

Quiz for the Vision Dynamic

1. Do you write weekly goals for what you want to accomplish?
   ❑ Yes   ❑ No

2. Do you write goals for what you want to accomplish this year, five years and 20 years down the road?
   ❑ Yes   ❑ No

3. Do you post your goals and rewards in a highly visible place?
   ❑ Yes   ❑ No

4. When setting goals, do you always have a reward established?
   ❑ Yes   ❑ No

5. Do you use *shaping* (i.e., positive reinforcement) in your professional and personal relationships?
   ❑ Yes   ❑ No

6. If so, do you take mental and physical possession of your reward—that is, do you find ways to see and touch your goals?
   ❑ Yes   ❑ No

7. Do you use an activity chart to track the flow of the necessary activities to achieve your monthly goal?
   ❑ Yes   ❑ No

8. Do you use a bar chart to track your monthly progress?
   ❑ Yes   ❑ No

9. Whenever possible, do you give your customers your product to hold, which will help them imagine owning the product?
   ❑ Yes   ❑ No

10. Do you use assumptive vocabulary to help your customers imagine themselves owning your product?
    ❑ Yes   ❑ No

11. Are you working at overcoming your own mental blocks or prejudices?
    ❑ Yes   ❑ No

12. Do you think of yourself as someone who will become successful, instead of as someone who will always have to financially struggle?

    ❑ Yes   ❑ No

13. Do you provide yourself—or if you are a manager, other employees—sales contests and incentives based on achieving excellence?

    ❑ Yes   ❑ No

14. Do you combine your Vision with Determination and work hard at achieving your goals?

    ❑ Yes   ❑ No

15. Do you imagine connecting with each your customers while working with them?

    ❑ Yes   ❑ No

16. Do you send thank-you notes to customers who don't buy that day?

    ❑ Yes   ❑ No

17. Are you instilling the importance of goals in your children?

    ❑ Yes   ❑ No

18. After reaching your monthly goals, do you set next month's goals right away?

    ❑ Yes   ❑ No

19. Are you able to break down your Vision into challenging yet achievable goals?

    ❑ Yes   ❑ No

20. Are you able to break down your goals into tasks?

    ❑ Yes   ❑ No

If you answered 18 to 20 yes's, you exhibit a high degree of dolphin-like Vision and will increase your success rapidly.

If you answered 13 to 17 yes's, beware—sharks are in the water with you.

If you answered 10 to 12 yes's, you are wounded and sharks are moving in.

If you answered nine or less yes's, *get out of the water*—you are about to be eaten alive!

Checklist for the Vision Dynamic

- Make goal-setting a regular part of your professional and personal life.
- Use *stationing* as a way of focusing and honing your energies toward reaching your goals.
- Whenever you set a goal, set a reward that is exciting, and post reminders in a highly visible place.
- Talk to yourself and others as if you will achieve and obtain your goals, even when you are not confident.
- Use lists to help you accomplish simple or complex projects with completion dates or times.
- Write down the areas in which you need to improve.
- Let your mind wander to help you move to the next plateau—professionally and personally.
- Chart your professional progress, comparing it to your goal each month.
- Divide your goals into tasks and use activity charts to monitor and keep you on track.
- Use follow-up phone calls to impress your customers and let them know that doing business with them is important to you.
- Involve your family in your professional goal-setting and the reward you will all receive *when* you accomplish the goal.
- Help your customers imagine themselves owning your product by using assumptive vocabulary, such as *"your* product," and by having *them* hold *their* product.
- Stay focused on your goals and visions by using visual reminders in places where you frequent often—your datebook, the refrigerator, your car...
- If you are a manager or business owner, use contests and incentives to increase sales immediately.
- Keep your goals realistic, qualitative and measurable—and always with your Vision in sight.
- Be sure to send a handwritten, personalized note to your customers right away—whether you get the sale that day or not.

In conclusion about Vision

When implemented, the techniques described in this section can bring you incredible achievement, a feeling of optimism and tremendous financial wealth. The human mind is like a missile. Give your mind a target, work at it and you will hit it. Without a goal, your mind will use its valuable energy searching for direction, fatally falling short of its target. Discipline yourself to become a goal-setter by using your Vision. Fully executing and mastering these techniques will be one of the best gifts you can ever give yourself.

Don't let any sharks get in your way. Remember, dolphins are smarter, quicker and stronger than sharks and they always hit their targets! Looking to the future is exhilarating and profitable!

Enjoy your Vision!

Dynamic Four: Enthusiasm

In this dynamic you will learn:

- How Enthusiasm will make you more appealing both professionally and personally!
- The correlation between Enthusiasm and success.
- How acting Enthusiastic all the time will increase your success in life.

"Nothing great was ever achieved without enthusiasm."
—Ralph Waldo Emerson

In my business experience, I have discovered that the top professionals in any field have one distinct thing in common—Enthusiasm. People are drawn to Enthusiastic people and businesses like magnets! When you allow yourself to become sincerely enthusiastic, *you* change and so do the people around you. Enthusiasm is an incredibly contagious emotion.

Most of us have been conditioned to act subdued and restrained in our professional dealings. We have effectively been robbed of our natural, childlike Enthusiasm—a loss felt on all aspects of our professional and personal lives. The more Enthusiasm and positive energy you can project, the more positively you will be received. Let me put this bluntly: Enthusiasm sells! It sells products, concepts and ideas! Stanford University did a study on sales success, that showed 15 percent of sales success was related to product knowledge—and 85 percent to Enthusiasm.

Everyone today appreciates the term "user-friendly." Making dynamic and powerful connections goes beyond being user-friendly—it requires us to be *customer-Enthusiastic!*

When dolphins want to interact with a human, they will often follow along in the water while the person is walking on the pier. They jump out of the water, bob up and down, click and whistle Enthusiastically—all to get attention. I can't imagine what else dolphins could do, that I haven't seen, to grab people's attention. They don't seem to have any concerns about being socially correct when it comes to Enthusiasm. This is a powerful lesson we can learn from them if we want to be as captivating as dolphins.

"I prefer the folly of enthusiasm to the indifference of wisdom."
—Anatole France, French author

If you present a positive, upbeat image to your customers or business contacts, you will have a better, more appealing image than your competition. This goes way beyond nice clothes and appealing letterhead (which are also important). It goes to the soul of the person, the product and the image. Enthusiasm is an elevation of the soul!

Make dynamic impressions with Enthusiastic gestures

In Dynamic Two: Instinct, we examined how Instinct assists you in understanding your customer—which assists you in making a connection. In this section we will examine how to make a splash in today's shark-infested business waters by communicating our Enthusiasm in gestures.

People "listen" to our actions far more than our words. We process information at three to four times the rate someone is speaking. In other words, we are able to "hear" a lot more than just the words. Dolphins, as we've already seen, have an exceptional ability for picking up on nonverbal cues. Humans have this ability, too, even though we often don't recognize it. Even though most of your customers and business associates have not received formal training on body language, they can undoubtedly read silent signals. They are sizing you up when they watch and listen to you. By examining your communication style—words and body language—thoroughly, you will uncover numerous opportunities to create a more dynamic connection with those around you.

Make your nonverbal message dynamic

If you normally stand while presenting your product or service, then stand *dynamically!* Use confident posture, strong eye contact and a dazzling smile! If you present your products or services sitting down, lean forward in your chair. Lean forward, using your own back to sit straight, not the back of the chair. This demonstrates your Enthusiasm, work ethic and strong interest in your customer. Otherwise you may be perceived as a sloppy, disinterested businessperson who is just going through the motions.

Albert Mehrabian conducted a now-famous study on how people interpret what you are telling them. According to Dr. Mehrabian, people interpret messages using three modes of communication—verbal, vocal and visual. (For more on this topic, read Mehrabian's book, *Silent Messages*.) The following chart illustrates how much of each mode can be attributed to the total message.

Mode of communication	Percent of message
Verbal (words)	7
Vocal (tone, pitch, etc.)	38
Visual (body language)	55

Verbal is your actual choice of vocabulary. One example is responding with slang. Do you say, "Yeah" or "Yes!"? Do you say, "It's *fine*" or "It's *great!*"?

Vocal is the way your voice *sounds*—your pitch, tone, enunciation. A word spoken in an upbeat, Enthusiastic tone will sound totally different than the same word spoken in a monotone voice. One example is "Hello." Depending upon your tone, it will translate as, *"Hi!* I am thrilled to meet you," or "Hello. I really wish I was somewhere else."

According to Mehrabian, body language is responsible for sending more than half of the message! Sometimes your mouth says one thing while your body says another. When people see you adjusting your clothes, fiddling and scratching, they become distracted by your message. Then they lose confidence in you.

Positive body language and your image

My husband and I recently watched an episode of the television news show "20/20." This edition showed how some people were being favored in different situations because they were more physically attractive. I feel strongly that having an excellent and professional image is very important and beneficial in business, so I was an interested observer of this episode.

To illustrate this point, the program set up two actresses dressed in identical clothing. Separately, each actress stood next to a broken-down vehicle looking as if they needed help. The more attractive actress received a much higher quantity and quality of assistance. In summation, the more attractive you are, the more likely you will be to receive the compassion, support and attention of others...right? Wrong! It was not the *body* of the more attractive actress that attracted people to her, it was a combination of her appearance and her body language!

The attractive actress used more open gestures and smiled more often. The less attractive actress used closed gestures such as crossing her arms, and she hardly ever smiled. This difference in gestures exaggerated the perceptions that were made about each actress.

Using positive body language will be more attractive to your business associates or customers and will help you make a dynamic connection. You can do many things to create a more attractive image and add significantly to a postive image.

Positive gestures for a dynamic image

1. **Smiling.** Smiling is one of the most effective nonverbal gestures you can employ to create a positive image. Look at the dolphins—they always look like they are smiling! That perpetual smile is one of the many reasons humans find them irresistible.

Make a conscious effort to smile. Studies show that most people smile a very small percentage of their day. Perhaps they don't smile because they don't feel they can smile while they are doing something else such as listening, speaking or reading. I assure you, if you want to be a top professional you can smile when you are listening, speaking or reading—and you must. Not an ear-to-ear fake smile, but a sincere "I'm interested" enthusiastic smile.

2. **Eye contact.** Without eye contact, smiling will not come across as confident as the combination of eye contact and smiling. The combination of smiling and eye contact is very powerful whether you are a man or woman. When you make eye contact with an individual, you are saying "I am interested, I want to and can help." When you don't establish eye contact, a person may subconsciously detect disinterest, preoccupation or, worse, dishonesty.

By eye contact I mean being interested enough to look at a person's eyes for at least five seconds at a time. Remember to smile; don't scowl, look mean or glare. Five seconds may seem like a long period of time at first, but the better you get, the longer you will be able to look at someone Enthusiastically, keeping their attention and building dynamic connections. If you are lucky enough to have a dolphin establish eye contact with you, as they often do, you will not forget that magic feeling.

3. **Nodding.** Head nodding is one of the best unkept secrets of body language that will help establish an Enthusiastic dynamic conversation. When someone is speaking, it might not be possible to verbally reconfirm and reassure him or her that you are listening and understanding. Head nodding is an important nonverbal gesture that can do both. Add a smile and maintain eye contact for added impact. When *you* are speaking, head nodding will subconsciously promote agreement and help persuade them to your point of view.

Don't forget that eye contact!

4. Open-handed gestures. The open hand, particularly the open palm, is still used for such solemn rituals as swearing in a courtroom. The opposite of the open-hand gesture is a tight-fisted palm. The fist conveys anger and hostility. You will immediately increase the power of your connection with people by making a conscious effort to use open-hand gestures when you communicate.

Open-hand gestures reflect honesty. Stories suggest that during peace treaties, Native American tribal leaders would hold up their open hands. This meant, "We come in peace, we have no weapons, you can trust us."

A universally understood gesture—approaching slowly with arms out and palms forward—makes the statement, "I come unarmed and mean no harm." Today, the handshake is used as an introduction; however, it started as a much more committed form of communication. It was originally used to seal a deal and make a vow. You should extend your hands palm forward in handshakes. This will communicate openness and trust.

Look at Allstate Insurance's advertisements. Allstate's logo is two open hands, an appropriate and powerful use of body language. The accompanying slogan is "You are in good hands with Allstate." The company uses this gesture because many people dislike or are skeptical when buying insurance—and it wants to communicate to potential and existing customers that Allstate is trustful and honest.

The use of open-hand gestures will help build credibility, which will be instrumental during the communication process.

5. **Touching.** Just as a handshake can initiate a positive connection with another, a gentle touch on the arm or a pat on the back can help reinforce that connection. I hear you thinking "sexual harassment." But we're not talking about *that* kind of touching. I am aware of and glad that the whole issue of sexual harassment has been addressed and is being dealt with in many businesses today. Sadly, we are in the unfortunate position of paying for the misconduct of others who have abused the privilege of touching—because appropriate forms of touching have been valuable in making magnetic connections. And in most venues it is still acceptable to "touch" through a handshake, a light pat on the shoulder or perhaps a gentle clasp to the forearm.

Here are a few guidelines, however:

- When working with a member of the opposite sex, be cautious about using touch as a communicative gesture. Handshakes are always appropriate. A touch to the sleeve or perhaps guiding the individual by gently holding the elbow or upper arm is generally "safe." But avoid any gestures that might be misconstrued.
- When working with a couple, it is advisable not to touch the individual of the opposite sex. In other words, if you're a woman working with a husband and wife, it is fine to shake both their hands, as well as lightly touch the woman's arm or shoulder. But don't use touch as a connecting gesture with the man.

Bo, my favorite dolphin, coming to greet me with open fins.

- Be sensitive to nonverbal feedback when you touch others. While your back-patting or arm-touching may be meant as a bonding gesture, some individuals may be uncomfortable because of cultural differences or narrower boundaries of personal space. If the person seems to stiffen or pull away, take a cue and keep your touching to a handshake.

Gestures to avoid

1. **Folded arms.** Folding your arms across your chest communicates to others that you are closed or defensive. Now you argue that it may just mean you are cold. My response is, why take a chance of communicating something else to a customer or business associate? My advice? If you're cold, start wearing long underwear. Do whatever it takes to free up your arms and hands so you can use them to express positive gestures to others, rather than keeping yourself warm.

2. **Hands in pockets.** Hands in the pockets are often interpreted as a sign of insecurity, sloppiness or suspicious behavior. When your hands are in your pockets they are not open and visible. Additionally, you probably have to slouch while your hands are in your pockets. This is a negative gesture to be avoided. Worse, still, is jingling the change in your pocket.

3. **Watch-checking.** During one of the 1992 presidential debates, President Bush used a gesture that haunted him. While in a debate with then-Governor Clinton and Ross Perot, President Bush looked at his watch numerous times. Top national publications interpreted this gesture and reported that President Bush was uncomfortable. They felt he wanted the debate to be over or that he had better things to do with his time. His image was damaged. People *watched* his gestures more than they listened to his words.

   Don't look at your watch unless you want to send the signal that it is time for your customers or clients to go away.

4. **Hiding behind barriers.** In the same debate mentioned above, Governor Clinton commanded powerful body language. He came out from behind the lectern regularly and used eye contact and open-hand gestures. President Bush seemed to realize what Governor Clinton was doing and came out from behind the lectern as well. However, when President Bush did come out from behind the lectern, he generally hung on to it. It appeared to be a security clutch.

   When you are working on making a connection with someone, come out from behind the counter or desk. Sit or stand next to the individual, almost face to face but slightly offset (depending on if they are sitting or standing). When you are confronted with an angry customer or disgruntled associate, walk around to the same side of the counter or table. The laws of human nature say that is where friends are...only enemies hide behind the barriers.

Other gestures or nonverbal posures to avoid include: turning your back on the person, touching or rubbing your neck (communicates frustration), pointing, looking at someone over your glasses (demeaning), rubbing your hands together (indicates greediness) or offering a limp handshake (appears weak and fragile).

How to exceed expectations

When I conduct customer service workshops for businesses across the country, I give each of the attendees a short quiz (see the example below). I always ask for their definitions of customer service. Unfortunately, I often get a pretty weak definition: "Customer service is serving the customers' needs." This is prehistoric!

Customer focus quiz

1. What is your definition of customer service?

2. How do you try to show each customer that they are important?

3. What could we do at our company to make our customers even happier with us?

The goal of a professional or progressive company must be to *exceed* the customers' needs and expectations—not just *meet* them! This means pleasantly surprising your customers—even dazzling them! When you do dazzle your customers, you are prompting the most powerful advertising of all—word-of-mouth referrals. This type of promotion is far less expensive and much more powerful than investing in the largest billboards, the cleverest jingles or even a full-page spread in *The New York Times*.

For a company to provide uniform, excellent customer service, each staff member must first know and understand the company's views on customer service. In today's shark-infested business waters, simply serving the customer is not enough. With the massive amount of advertising competing for customers' attention, they know they have plenty of options. And they will go elsewhere if they are not enthusiastic about the service they receive from you. Exceeding customer expectations will help ensure that you gain repeat business and, better yet, word-of-mouth advertising.

Create an attention-grabbing greeting

Your customers are inundated by countless advertising messages. To be successful in today's business environment, you need to set yourself apart—and quickly. I am among the countless others who've found great success by using dynamic greetings and attention-grabbers. This will assist you in setting yourself apart from the competition and making a dynamic connection.

How many times have you walked into a place of business and then tried unsuccessfully to attract the attention of someone? I wonder where they take those classes in eye-contact evasion. No matter how hard you try, their eyes seem to look right past you. Yet someone else, without a word, can use a positive gesture and a smile to let you know they will be right with you! You relax and enjoy your visit.

You've heard it said that you never have a second chance to make a good first impression. Your initial contact, or greeting, is so important whether you're welcoming a customer or visitor, or whether you're on a job interview.

The following is some advice on developing and polishing your "greeting skills" to maximize your business connections.

- Prepare!
- Plan on liking and being interested in your customer and imagine that the customer is a friend.
- Relax, yet be attentive and ready to act on a customer's behalf.
- Make the individual feel welcome—by smiling.
- Use positive eye contact. Look right at your customer. (If you are on the phone, imagine you can see the individual.)
- Compliment your customer.

- Make an effort to learn your customer's name—and use it. I do this by extending my hand and introducing myself. This prompts the person to give me his or her name. The use of an individual's name has sort of a magical power to it. It turns an impersonal business transaction into a personal, even friendly, encounter.
- Develop and use an attention-grabbing opener. (Read on for examples.)

A powerful handshake makes a dynamic greeting

Most people respond favorably to an effective handshake. Your hand-shake says a lot about you, so make sure it says what you want it to say! Your handshake should be firm, but not overpowering (like your business style!).

Shaking hands allows you to get closer to your customer or business associate. It affords the opportunity to make a dynamic connection. Take advantage by developing your handshake. Here are some hints:

- Bending your elbow a bit when offering your hand puts you into more of a personal zone rather than a strained, public zone. (I am not recommending you get within inches of them—that would be too close.) Now you are close enough to start breaking down the barriers of discomfort quickly.
- When offering your hand, direct it upward. This is another opportunity to display your palm (subconsciously promoting openness and trustworthiness).

Letitia Baldrige on handshakes

Because there is so much controversy on the proper etiquette of hand-shakes I consulted with renowned protocol expert Letitia Baldrige for the latest information. She is the author of many books on manners. She has been the protocol expert for the White House and for embassies around the world. Here are a few pointers from Ms. Baldrige:

"You can never shake hands too often in business. It's a physical bonding. It helps to have a good handshake. Practice with friends and family members who will be frank with you and who'll tell you if your handshake is warm and friendly, but not too aggressive. Be sure your handshake is neither clammy nor bone-crushing nor limp, as though the other person were clasping a cold, dead fish. Unless you're on the street in freezing weather, remove your right-hand glove before handshaking.

"The usual rule of thumb in whose hand to shake first when meeting business colleagues is logical: Shake the hand of the person nearest you first, and then shake the hand of everyone else in the group. It's proper protocol to shake the senior person's hand first. But if you don't know who is senior to whom, just go ahead and shake the nearest hand.

"If two people are standing there, only one of whom you know, shake first that person's hand, who, in turn, should introduce the other person to you. If this doesn't happen, your friend may have forgotten the other person's name and doesn't wish to admit it. So go ahead and greet the other person there, shaking his or her hand and stating your name.

"If you are greeting a couple you know, shake either person's hand first. The etiquette of 'always the woman first' no longer holds. The important thing for everyone to remember is to get out that hand and make the other person feel you are a friendly person who's nice to know.

"If you and your spouse are out with business colleagues on a social occasion, remember to make sure that every spouse meets every other spouse. If you and your spouse stick out your hands, the others will extend theirs, too, hopefully stating their names at the same time. Don't worry about who should extend the hand first. It's much more important just to get out that hand— unless you meet the Queen of England, in which case you don't put out your hand unless she comes up to you and gives you her hand (not much chance of that, is there?).

"If you are going around shaking hands with several people in a group and a child is among them, don't forget to shake the child's hand, too. (I remember JFK told me once that when he

was campaigning for president, he couldn't even count the number of babies' fists he had shaken; otherwise he might have had to kiss all the babies, which could have been bad for the babies, bad for their mothers—who worry about germs—and bad for the presidential candidate, who might have immediately contracted the baby's sniffles.)"

Dynamic attention-grabbing openers

The first words the customer, client or business visitor hears when coming to your place of business should convey an enthusiastic welcome and build the foundation of a dynamic connection. When developing your attention-grabbing openers, whether you're developing them for your sole use or as a manager, to establish a proper greeting for other employees, you should give careful thought to the message and image you want to convey. While such greetings should always seem natural, it's appropriate to "script" them or at least provide a framework or guidelines in order to be most effective.

For example, at the drive-through at my Rochester McDonald's, I was greeted with, "Thank you for choosing McDonald's." What are they really saying? "We know you have a choice. We appreciate your choosing us!"

Attention-grabbing greetings can be nonverbal, as well. Wegmans, a highly progressive regional grocery retailer, uses the motto, "Wegmans, where every day you get our best!" This is written on huge signs as you enter their building, on their uniforms and even on their bags and balloons.

"May I help you?" While a traditional query from a salesperson, receptionist or customer service representative, this is certainly not a dynamic or enthusiastic way to greet an individual. Its other major weakness is that it results in a *yes* or *no*—and probably a *no*. Your greeting should convey, in addition to a welcoming spirit, an openness to connect and a willingness to communicate. You should, therefore, use dynamic, open-ended, attention-grabbing greetings.

- "Thank you for coming in today! How may I help you?"
- "Welcome! What brings you in today?"

- "I'd be happy to help you! How can I be of assistance?"
- "Thank you for coming in today. What can I do to help?"
- "Welcome to the Smith Company. Where may I direct you?"
- "Good morning. What may I help you find today?

After your initial exchange

- "You picked a great day to come in! We are running a sale on our fitness machines."
- "We are Chicago's largest computer store, yet we pride ourselves on individual assistance."
- "You picked a terrific day to come in; we just received our new fall line of merchandise."
- "You will be glad you stopped in! We have one of the finest lines of widgets in the Valley."
- "We carry Brand X and Brand Y products, which have ranked as superior choices by *Consumer Reports* for the last four years. I'd be happy to show them to you."
- Proudly inform customers of the product specifics that will benefit them the most. "Based on the fact that you were using this for business purposes, you may be interested to know that it has Windows '95 already built in, which has proven highly beneficial to other business owners. By the way, what type of business are you in?"
- Quickly ask an open-ended question that will encourage the customer to converse with you. "How long have you been in business?" (Don't ask, "Have you been in business long?", which will result in a yes or no answer.)

Phone calls

- "Thank you for choosing ABC Company! How may I help you?"
- "Thank you for calling ABC Company! Where may I direct your call?"

- "Mr. Jones, I'm sure that John will be pleased to speak with you. Unfortunately he has stepped away from his desk. I will be happy to let him know you called. At what number can he reach you?"

When a customer must wait for service

- "You are welcome to wait, Mr. Jones. We have a comfortable waiting area, with complimentary coffee. Were you aware we have a '60 minutes or it's free' guarantee?"

When greeting your most important customers: your family

- "I've had a great day and I can't wait to hear all about your day. You go first!"

Greetings that translate to "good riddance!"

Whether you communicate in words or gestures, your customers or guests will know whether your greeting is sincere. If otherwise, you might as well post a sign on the door that says, "Visitors Unwelcome." Avoid the following in order to make your greetings dynamic:

- Thinking about all the other work you could be doing if this customer were not here.
- Grouping or huddling with other employees while customers are in your place of business. They will think they are an intrusion instead of the only reason you opened your doors this morning.
- Reading newspapers at work. I don't care if you are reading *The Wall Street Journal*—it *looks* like you are goofing off.
- Leaning on counters. You look like you are bored.
- Giving negative verbal responses. For example, "Oh, this isn't my department," or "I'm on break," when approached by a customer. Or "I'll be with you as soon as I get rid of this other customer."

Practice while hectic

It is all good and well to imagine yourself giving your brilliant smile and dynamic greeting in the perfect setting: all your other work done, no other customers needing your attention, your spouse has dinner under way and no challenges with your children. (I'm still waiting for this magic moment to happen.)

Why is it that customers seem to come into your company and the phone will ring when you are already insanely busy? (Remember, this is a good thing. When I hear businesspeople complain that it's too busy, I always respond with, "That's great!") Regardless, practice your Enthusiastic greetings, imagining that you are juggling customers and tasks. Using an Enthusiastic greeting, especially when it is hectic, lets customers know that they are important.

Congratulations! Now you know how to create a positive first impression whether with a client, customer, new boss, new employee or business associate. But your job is not over! You need to harness that Enthusiasm, plus other skills, in order to build on that connection.

Beyond the greeting: more steps to establishing connections

Sometimes, knowing why people don't listen will help you form your strategy to bring them into a listening frame of mind. Here are some reasons people don't listen:

- **Message overload.** When you spend most of the day listening, you simply put too much information into your brain to retain all of it. By connecting with your customer, your customers will tune into you instead of tuning you out.

- **No perceived benefit.** The listener does not recognize the advantages to buying your product or utilizing your service. Usually this is because the message has not been customized to fit the individual's specific needs. That's why it's so important to target your message to the interests of your customer—and to deliver it with Enthusiasm.

- **Preoccupation.** Perhaps the person had a fight with his or her spouse, missed lunch or has pressing business at work that is causing distractions. Remembering that the words we speak can only take up 25 to 35 percent of a person's total mental capabilities at any given moment, it is your responsibility to keep the individual focused on you. By using Enthusiastic gestures, words and tones, you'll make it easier for your customer to focus on you.

- **Other distractions.** Loud or irritating noises, interruptions from others and a crowded or uncomfortable environment may distract a person, making him or her an unlikely recipient of your message. It's important to do whatever you can to help the person focus on what you're saying, even if it means moving him or her to another, quieter location.

- **Hearing problems.** Nearly 50 percent of all people have hearing problems—50 percent! That, coupled with other noise, distractions and roadblocks to communication, means you've got a real challenge to get your message across. If you suspect an individual is hard of hearing, you'll have to work doubly hard to connect. Your nonverbal gestures and eye contact will be doubly important.

  When working with deaf patients, dolphins become more animated than normal by bobbing more, establishing intense eye contact and even splashing. It's as if they are keeping their new friend involved by relying on the other senses more. Great advice for us, but please don't throw water at your customers.

Compliments: a sure path to dynamic connections

Offering sincere compliments is another effective route to making dynamic connections. It is so rare for folks to receive a sincere compliment (unfortunately) that it often catches them off guard and grabs their attention. People are not accustomed to receiving compliments. It helps them feel more comfortable with the surroundings and with you.

There are some things that are better to compliment than others. In a retail situation, try to compliment something that has a parallel to your product. For example, if you sell car audio equipment or cellular phones, try to notice what kind of car your customer pulled up in. Then you would be able to sincerely compliment something you liked about the car: the model, color, etc. Or if a woman has a particularly nice hairstyle and you sell clothing, you could say something like, "I'd like to show you our new fall line of turtlenecks. The colors and style will really emphasize your great hairstyle."

In many sales situations, jewelry is one of the safest and best things to compliment. People are usually quite proud of their jewelry. For women, compliment a ring or earrings; for men, compliment a watch. If someone is wearing a substantial amount of jewelry, that person is often trying to make a statement—"Hey, look at me"—so by all means do so!

In addition to jewelry, for men, I look for a nice tie, suit or sweater. Once I mistakingly complimented a man's tie when he was with his wife. I realized that the compliment might have seemed suggestive— as if I had other interests in him. So I quickly recovered by turning to his wife and asking, "Did you pick that out for him?" She appreciated being included.

As a woman complimenting another woman, I may compliment an attractive haircut, a purse, scarf or perhaps a sweater.

A man should generally stay away from complimenting a woman's clothing. I don't think I need to warn you that under no condition should a man or woman compliment any particular part of the anatomy.

In management situations, compliment a behavior or action you are trying to duplicate. These would include the neatness of an office for an office manager, the neatness or timeliness of paperwork of a sales-person or the promptness of delivery of a vendor.

The children of the adults with whom you are trying to connect should be seen—and heard and complimented! No matter how much your tolerance is being tested, if you react with frustration you may as well write off whatever you are trying to accomplish with the parent. Even if the parent agrees that their child is being a little terror, he or she will most often transfer that annoyance right over to you! Don't pretend you don't see them pouring coffee on your briefcase. Do find the humor in the situation and laugh.

Of course, it is far easier to compliment children if they are behaving. So to encourage them to behave, have things to keep them occupied. Try coloring books, crayons or videos. The parents will appreciate a few moments to be able to concentrate and relax. Please notice that I do not refer to children as "kids." It's fine if you prefer to call your children "kids." But some parents will be offended by the term.

If you are in someone's office, there is a wealth of information to help you connect, and a compliment is an excellent way to start. Look for and compliment fine furniture, artwork or a particular book you see on the shelf.

Establishing common ground

To make your interaction with someone dynamic, first look for some common ground on which the two of you can stand. People want to be able to trust you—and they are looking for signs that show them they can. Such commonalities offer a feeling of security. They help show your customer that you are not a stranger and, therefore, less of a threat.

How many times were you told as a child not to talk to strangers? Commonalities help communicate an important message to others: "Look, I am not a stranger to you! I understand things you understand. I like things you like."

Finding common ground requires Determination, Instinct, Vision and, of course, an Enthusiastic delivery. Recently, I was working out in the field with a trainee one of my clients asked me to work with. His presentation was heavily product-based. I told him how important it was to make a dynamic connection. He asked me to show him. On the next call, we were with a customer who just moved in the area. I enthusiastically asked, "Oh? Where are you from?" They moved from Boston. "I love Boston! My favorite aunt lives there and it's a great city. I enjoy visiting. Where in Boston are you from?" She was thrilled and we talked about it for a few minutes. Connection! Common ground, or shall I say friendly waters? This helped her see me as a friendly dolphin rather than a shark.

There are many ways to find a common ground from which you can begin your connection. It requires keeping your eyes and ears open, looking for clues of commonality. Here are a few to get you started:

- Look for sports team logos on T-shirts, jackets or caps. A comment about a favorite team can often create a bond.

- Observation of other apparel as well as bags or other items the person might be carrying will offer further clues: "I see you've been shopping at that new boutique. I've been wanting to get over there. What do you think about their selection?" Or, "I love that pin. I collect art deco pieces, but I've never seen anything as unusual as that."

- *Place* is always an easy connector. If an individual has recently moved from or otherwise indicates he or she has connections to a location, you have an opportunity for common ground. "I grew up in Jersey. You're from Paramus? I lived in Ho-Ho-Kus!" "We were in Napa Valley just last year! It's beautiful in the fall." Even, "You just got back from Mexico? I've always wanted to go there. What did you think?"

Likability

People who don't like you won't buy from you. It's as simple as that. They also won't hire you, nor will they perform well if you hire them. All this should be rather obvious. Yet, people too often fail to factor in the impact of likability. A wrongheaded approach in any field.

Despite their obvious power and superior connection skills, dolphins are almost always friendly in their dealings. That is one important reason they are so well-loved and admired.

Recently, a major medical journal reported a study that sought to determine why some doctors are more prone to lawsuits than others. Researchers found that doctors who are not well-liked by their patients are three times more likely to be sued than those who are well-liked.

Are doctors who get sued any less competent than their colleagues who manage to stay out of court? Apparently not. The data showed that patients who liked their physician's bedside manner and felt well-treated by office staff rarely sought relief in court. If likability is a key factor in a patient's assessment of a physician's proficiency, imagine how it affects the way people evaluate *your* performance.

I'm not suggesting that you smile and treat people well to cover up a lack of competence or quality work. I simply want you to understand that people who like you will be motivated to help and give you what you want.

Ultimately, the question is not one of competence vs. kindness, but of how hard you are willing to work to do that which may not come easy.

Use humor to make dynamic connections

Dolphins have a tremendous sense of humor. Ladies, if you ever swim with a dolphin, do not swim with a two-piece swimsuit—as one female visitor at the DRC in Florida learned the hard way! AJ, a dolphin who loved to play pranks, untied the back of her top and swam away with it. The woman remained in the water while the trainer, trying to keep a straight—averted—face, called to AJ, "That's it! Go get it!" and gave the command. The dolphin started to return with the bathing suit top. All of a sudden he tossed it in the mangrove patch where no one could reach it! AJ giggled, clicked and whistled as if in hysterics. Finally, all of us, the trainer and woman included, dissolved into laughter, thoroughly entertained by AJ's antics.

Another time, I was talking with a friend while sitting on one of the floating docks. Suddenly, AJ jumped up out of the water—just to surprise me! As he startled me, he giggled. He must have been waiting for just the right moment when he'd get the most bang out of his surprise. Afterward, he proceeded to bring me presents as if to make up to me—mangrove leaves (which I certainly treasured). But he knows the greatest gift he gives is the joy and laughter his silly jokes bring to everyone he shares his humor with.

One of the first characteristics of getting old is the loss of our ability to play. Did you know a 5-year-old laughs 500 times a day? Adults laugh only about 15 times a day. The people we find most popular—whether businesspeople or friends, are those who make us laugh. Humor is contagious. What a wonderful gift to give to all those who touch your life.

"The true genius of living is to carry the spirit of the child into old age."

—Norman Vincent Peale,
paraphrasing Aldous Huxley, British author

Safe humor

Humor is a wonderful connection tool. But be extremely careful of sarcasm—it can be dangerous. For example, your favorite customer walks in, you notice their hair is in an odd hairstyle, you say with a laugh, "Geez! Bad hair day?" They might seem okay, but most likely you just hurt their feelings. In addition to sarcasm, it is wise to stay away from humor that ridicules appearance, race, ethnic origin, politics or sex, for example.

You are generally safer to target yourself rather than others. Let's say you are handing someone something and he or she drops it. Instead of saying, "Klutz!," I would recommend saying something like, "They don't call me butterfingers for nothing!" You both laugh and they appreciate your graceful handling of a difficult situation.

How to cope in an unenthusiastic environment

It is often difficult to maintain your Enthusiasm when everyone around you is dismal and depressed. However, Enthusiasm can be contagious. If you can hang on to that positive attitude despite the gloom around you, you may inspire others to become Enthusiastic.

If that doesn't work? Go someplace else. Just as your Enthusiasm might be contagious, negativism is catching, too—especially if it's the pervasive attitude in your workplace. As the saying goes, "If you lay down with dogs, you'll get up with fleas." If you surround yourself with negative people, you may become negative yourself.

Just after I started my training career, I slipped on ice in my doorway, hit my head on a glass door and proceeded to fall face first into the jagged glass, virtually cutting off my nose and puncturing tendons in my arm. The plastic surgeon asked what I did for a living. I explained, "I'm a professional trainer and speaker." He said, "You don't do that anymore; I don't think your nose can be saved." I found a new plastic surgeon. I feared this doctor's negative attitude would rub off on me, impeding the healing process. I very much enjoyed proving him wrong. My nose, although touchy for a while, stayed intact and there are only minor reminders of the accident.

As Norman Cousins, author of *Anatomy of an Illness,* said about the thousands who successfully fight cancer and other fatal illnesses, "Don't deny the diagnosis. Try to defy the verdict." When your co-workers have the disease of negativism, try to cure them. If it doesn't work, avoid the plague they are spreading.

Spread your Enthusiasm

Often, your Enthusiasm will help bring others into a better frame of mind. Your example can help turn the whole company in a better direction. The following are just a few ways you can spread Enthusiasm in your work environment:

- Embrace change and new developments with optimism. "I'm really looking forward to this new product line. I can't wait to get it. How about you?"
- Find a little way to make someone's day more pleasant.
- When someone is complaining, change the subject to something positive. If this doesn't work, move on.
- Use an Enthusiastic, can-do vocabulary when talking about work.

If you're in a management position, implement a small award program that rewards the employee with the most positive attitude. Have the employees vote themselves. The reward can be something as simple as movie passes. Surprise the winner with a banner generated from a computer or a bunch of balloons with a note such as "Thanks for brightening our day." This is another powerful form of *shaping*. You should almost immediately notice most of the employees improving their behaviors and then attitudes.

Don't get discouraged if staff and co-workers don't start reacting positively right away—it may take awhile. But your efforts will be well worth it if you are able to convert a negative group into an enthusiastic one.

Can-do vocabulary

One way to pump up Enthusiasm among co-workers is to employ a can-do vocabulary—using languange that leaves the listener in a positive and Enthusiastic state of mind. This is a skill that will take some practice and effort on your part. But the payoff is well worth the effort, as you will have developed a very powerful skill. In addition, using positive, can-do vocabulary is a wonderful way to help you turn up your own Enthusiasm!

Words have a certain power—they conjure up very specific images in our minds. To illustrate this point during my training seminars, I ask participants to think of "powerful" and "fluffy" things. You can't call a little fuzzy bunny rabbit "powerful," or a Lear Jet "fluffy."

Another example: When you hear the word "problem," what do you think of? Do you tighten up? Don't you just kind of cringe inside? You get stressed immediately. That word should be removed from your vocabulary. Replace the word "problem" with "situation," "challenge" or even "opportunity." When someone comes to you with a "problem," try saying this: "I would be happy to help you, what is the situation?" And boy, does that take the wind right out of the issue!

Another word to erase from our workplace vocabulary—"policy." I sat in a store the other day and heard a business representative say, "Well, that's our policy." I couldn't believe it. I wanted to shake her! It sends a message to customers, "Sorry, you're just a number and we're the store. We're important and you're not. This is the way it's going to be." Communicators and businesses with this attitude soon won't need to worry about all those rotten customers bothering them with "problems." They'll all be going to the competitors!

"How are you?"

What is your answer when someone asks you, "How are you?" Almost everyone in today's world will reply, "Fine," "Okay," or if we are lucky, "Good." If you are trying to make a connection with someone, "Fine" is not going to get you very far! Instead, respond *Enthusiastically* with:

- "I'm *great!* How are you?"
- "I'm *terrific!* How are you?"
- "I'm *excellent!* How are you?"

Remember, people are drawn to Enthusiastic people and businesses like magnets! And when their first impression of you is one of Enthusiasm, you're off to an *excellent* start.

During my sales training seminars, I always explain that starting off on an Enthusiastic note is critical to making a connection. Janet, a salesperson attending a seminar, complained that she felt uncomfortable answering in this fashion. "Don't you find such words to be disingenuous?" she asked. I politely explained that the point was to work on becoming sincerely Enthusiastic, and that these answers would prompt her to do so. "Having a positive, energetic response entails a certain amount of risk," I noted. "It may not be easy to adapt to this new approach in the beginning. You first have to be willing to shed old habits and replace them with better ones."

Janet didn't respond verbally, but I could tell by her body language that she was highly skeptical. I was left with the impression of a person unwilling to improve if it meant having to endure the least bit of discomfort. My suspicions were confirmed when I checked the performance record of the seminar participants. It turned out that Janet was one of the lower producers in her company. I was hardly surprised.

It was break time for the workshop participants I was working with. We'd just finished a preliminary discussion about Enthusiastic greetings. As the participants were walking out of the training room and into the hall, a hotel staff person walked in to refresh the room. He asked the participants that were milling out the door, "How are you doing?" Knowing that I was behind them, the group looked over their shoulders, and simultaneously and Enthusiastically responded with a roaring "Great!" He was impressed, even intrigued, and asked, "Why?" Much to my chagrin, the attendees looked at me and said, "We haven't gotten that far yet." A group of comedians. I was thinking, thank goodness this training session isn't over yet. We obviously have a few more points to cover!

One of the biggest compliments you can receive is when someone asks you why you are "great," "terrific" or "excellent." This means they heard you, you set yourself apart, and they are interested in hearing more. I recommend you follow up with more "can-do" vocabulary:

- "It's great to be here today!"
- "I'm pleased to meet with you today!"
- "Business is great!"
- "I'm glad to be here today."
- "I enjoy what I do."
- "It's a great day."

"How's work?"

Do you take your Enthusiastic attitude about your work to parties with you? When someone outside of work asks you how your business is going, do you reply with some version of, "Could be better," or "Oh, it's all right."

When you want to use a company or service, would you want to hire one that you felt "could be better" or that was just "all right"? No! If *you* think or, worse, say that the company "could be better" or is just "all right," then people will be leery of doing business with you. You may be a major cause in spreading a negative attitude about your company, just from your casual references.

Think of Enthusiastic responses, instead. You can be honest and still say something positive and encouraging about the situation at work.

Let's say business has been less than great lately. You might still be able to use one of the following:

- "Business is moving along."
- "I'm working hard and gaining a lot of valuable experience."
- "It's keeping me very busy."

Tom Hopkins (sales speaker and author) suggests that if you can't say, "Work is great!", say "Business is unbelievable!" (It covers it either way).

Say, "Yes!"

When opportunities come your way, don't even hesitate: Say, "Yes!" Recently I needed assistance with a project and needed it completed by noon of that same day. I asked two people for help. The first person responded with, "Yeah, I guess." The second, Julie, responded "Absolutely!" Guess which person I trusted with the project and who continues to truly impress me and has received merit increases in pay? By answering positively, you are displaying a can-do attitude and you will become more successful because your customers will know you can get the job done.

Turn dismal responses into dynamic dialogue!

Frequently in the course of our business days, we have to deal with "problems," or as we now Enthusiastically refer to them, *situations* or *challenges*. And while that situation may originate from a negative situation, our responses—if positive and Enthusiastic—can transform them into positive situations. Following are a number of dismal traditional responses to such situations, with recommended replacement phrases that will produce more positive results for you.

"Sorry about that..."

Occasionally, no matter how hard you try, unfortunately something will go wrong from time to time. For example, let's say you own a restaurant and are adequately staffed under normal conditions. Then a bus filled with 100 hungry people breaks down in front of your restaurant and all of them decide to join you for dinner, putting your people to the test. Even though everyone is moving as quickly as possible, customers become irritated because no one is available to take care of them quickly enough.

Granted, it would have been ideal to have enough people to take care of each customer quickly. But what do you do? An insincere "I'm sorry" is not enough and will certainly not turn a negative situation into a positive one. When you hear such a response, what do *you* think? I always think, "Sure you are!"

Another goal when responding to a complaint is to try to emphasize a positive outcome. You can accomplish this by mentioning a positive first. Here are a few suggested responses to a complaint:

- "I'm happy to help you now. I apologize for the delay."
- "Let's take care of that right now; I'd be happy to help you and I'm sorry for the confusion."
- "I will be happy to take care of this right now, and I apologize for any inconvenience."

Notice all responses emphasize resolution of the situation *now*. In addition, each response begins with the positive resolution and concluded with the apology. Each communicates to the respondent that the individual is sincerely sorry for the situation and is committed to finding an immediate solution.

"That's not my job."

We all know the frustration of calling a business with a problem and being told, "You've reached the wrong department," or trying to find a salesperson to answer a question and being told, "That's not my department." As a representative of a company or store, you must assume responsibility for the satisfaction of a customer—even if it is a situation you can't directly resolve. "But how?" you ask. It's easy! Simply assume responsibility for delivering the customer into the hands of someone you *know* can resolve the situation, even if you can't. Consider these responses:

- "Yes, we can certainly take care of that. Let me walk you over to the customer service center and get this resolved."
- "Let's fix that right now! I'll take your phone number and have the person in charge of that get right back to you."
- "Yes! We need to take action on that. Let me track down the head of that department for you right now."
- "Julie would be pleased to help you. She is assisting another customer right now. Let me get your phone number, and I'll have her call you back within a half-hour."

Notice that each response begins in a positive, can-do way. The individual assumes responsibility for getting the issue resolved, whether taking the customer to another department, or having another employee respond. In no case did the individual put the burden back on the customer, even to say, "Call so-and-so," or "Go over to that department."

"You'll have to call back later."

You've undoubtedly heard this response or a version of it: "Would you mind calling back?" "She's at lunch. You can call back in about an hour." "He's out sick today. Try tomorrow." Would I mind calling back? As a customer, I've often felt like shouting back, "Yes, I bloody well mind calling back!" It should never be the responsibility of the customer to call back! It is the company's responsibility to resolve the customer's situation or answer a question or take an order as soon as possible. You were fortunate they called you in the first place—especially if it was to give you the opportunity to fix a situation. If another person in the company cannot help the customer, then the employee who receives the call should take a message. Here are some more appropriate responses:

- "Lois isn't available now. May I be of assistance?"
- "I'd be happy to assist you myself. Please tell me how I can help."
- "Jim is not available now. Let me get your name and number and I'll have him return your call as soon as he's free."
- "Mrs. Johnson is out of the office. I'd be happy to ask one of the other customer service representatives to assist you."
- "I will walk this down to accounting myself, when they return at 1:30. Where can I reach you this afternoon?"

"If we have them, they'll be on the shelf."

One of my personal, all-time pet-peeve responses from a salesperson in a store is, "If they're not on the shelf, then we're probably out of them," or some such variation. What do I hear when they say this? "Gosh, you are really dumb! Besides I am busy, I don't have time to help an unimportant person like you. Go away!" If you've found yourself, as a salesperson, thinking such thoughts about your customers, consider this: Your store is unfamiliar, perhaps large and overwhelming to the customer. He or she may not understand the arrangement of the departments or categorization of merchandise. He or she may also be in a hurry. In addition, some merchandise often does get misplaced. Again, you as a store representative must assume responsibility for responding to the customers' needs. Here are a few more appropriate responses to consider:

- "Those should be on the shelf. Let me help you look for that!"
- "I'd be happy to help you look."
- "There don't appear to be any on the shelf. Let me see if I can find any in back."

"I'm not sure." "I could try." "Maybe." How often have you heard a person trying to assist someone say, "I could try to get that information to you by, maybe, Friday—if that's okay? I mean, if you want me to?" Language softeners such as *might, could, I'll have to check* and *maybe* result in watered-down communication. Avoid them!

What causes a person to use such wishy-washy vocabulary? Usually, uncertainty or discomfort. True, sometimes you won't know how you can resolve a customer's situation and you don't want to promise something you can't deliver. Say a client asks you to deliver a product by a certain date. You may not have the power to authorize that. But you *do* have the power to assure an answer by a certain date or time. There are ways to communicate dynamically and positively—even when you're not sure:

- "I will have an answer for you by Friday. Would 3 or 4 p.m. be a good time for you?"
- "I'll call you by the end of the day to confirm how we can proceed."
- "I will have your information by Thursday. When is better for us to review it together, Thursday morning or Thursday afternoon?"
- "I'll get an approval on this and get back to you within 24 hours."

And when you're following up or contacting a client or customer, keep the "soft" language out of your speech. While you may think it sounds humble to make statements such as "I was hoping..." or "If it would be okay with you..." this doesn't help you to come across in an Enthusiastic, dynamic way. If you act like an insignificant, unimportant person, you are going to be treated like one!

Instead try: "John Smith, please! This is Laura Laaman!" (Spoken as if Laura Laaman means something to him, even if it doesn't yet.) I've often had a receptionist from an organization I've never spoken with before respond with, "Oh, okay!" When you sound like you must be important, others just assume they should have recalled your name. It's all in your dynamic delivery!

"The difference between the right word and the almost right word is the difference between lightning and the lightning bug."
—Mark Twain

Speak in layman language—don't be too technical

There is a downside to having a thorough knowledge of your product or services. The advantage is that you will be prepared to answer any questions completely. This builds credibility and impresses your customers, clients or business associates. The negative is that you will exhaust and bore them if you go into too much unwanted detail!

I have found that many people (particularly men—sorry, guys) give out way too much technical information. Be sensitive to this: Use your Instincts to determine if you're losing your audience. Are their eyes wandering? Are they tapping their fingers? Are they turning away from you? Rarely will others stop you and tell you they don't understand what you're talking about. No one wants to appear ignorant, so people will let you continue, but they are thinking of ways to escape your presence!

Want to further aggravate the situation? Ask, "Do you understand?" Or, "Do you follow?" Rarely will someone answer truthfully if they don't. Instead, they'll mumble yes, but will feel further alienated from you. If you sense you're losing your listener, stop and try one of these responses (and remember to smile!):

- "I'm sorry! I get so excited about our products and the terrific benefits they bring our customers, I get carried away. What specifics can I tell you about them?"

- "That was more than any sane person would want to know about this! Tell me about how you might use this?"

- "Uh oh, now I'm even boring myself! Tell me, what made you want to look at this model?"

Please don't misunderstand me. I'm not suggesting that you refrain from offering important technical information. Sometimes this information is critical to the individual's decision. It may even be required by law for you to disclose certain facts. Just make sure you offer it in a way that the individual can understand and appreciate.

Explore your product for features, advantages and benefits

On a regular basis, salespeople, customer service people, managers and owners should list the strengths of their products and services. Why on a regular basis? This will keep them fresh in your mind. Because as you grow, these points will change and your list will grow. Keep your list close by so you can refer to it. Try keeping the list in a place you will see it often—in your day planner, address book or by the phone.

One progressive retailer took this idea and ran with it. He owns five large local appliance stores. This owner learned that a national chain was coming into town. Rather than focus on the negatives of the situation, such as the fact that he could not compete solely on price, he decided to take the proactive position of displaying large signs that boldly presented the benefits from buying at his store (not mentioning the competition). The signs and training he provided helped his employees communicate these benefits to his customers—allowing him to thrive in a highly competitive situation.

If your customers don't understand the benefits of using your company's products and services, they may choose another supplier. Customers are not mind-readers. Your employees, advertising, signs and marketing materials need to inform your customers of the advantages of doing business with you.

Many people are instructed upon and therefore familiar with the features of a product or service, but few people are good at communicating the benefits. That's unfortunate because people buy benefits, not features. *Features* are specific characteristics of the product or service. The *advantage* is what the characteristic does and the *benefit* is what it means to the customer. Customers buy benefits. The best way to communicate the benefits of your product or service is, after you state the feature and advantage, to begin your next sentence with *"So, what this means to you is..."* and then complete the sentence with something that you feel will appeal to your customer.

For example: Let's say you are a computer salesperson assisting a customer who is purchasing a computer to help his new business. I would recommend: "This new computer comes with Windows, which will make it easy to run all of your software. What this means to you is that it will increase the efficiency and productivity of your business." After all, that is why he is interested in buying a computer in the first place.

This is very different from simply saying, "This computer comes with Windows!" like it means something. Many salespeople make the mistake of assuming that this or any benefit will mean something to your customer. Just because Windows means something to you, it may mean nothing to your customer. You've had weeks, months or years to fully understand its meaning. Your customer hasn't.

To be successful, you should emphasize the *benefits* of your product, service or idea because it is the benefits that matter to us when making a decision. We don't buy a sofa because it has been coated with a protective treatment. We don't even buy it because resists the toughest stains. We buy it because it means we can watch videos and eat pizza with the kids on it, without worrying about ruining the upholstery.

The dynamic professional understands why people make decisions and constantly considers what is beneficial about his or her product or ideas. Never assume, however, just because you are so familiar with the benefits, that they may be obvious to others. Use Enthusiasm and excitement to point out the benefits to your customers, clients or business associates.

Often, we may be too close to our product, service or idea to think through how it will benefit the user. First, consider how these sales philosophers viewed the issue:

> *"Customers don't buy things. They buy tools to solve problems."*
> —Ted Levit, Harvard Business School,
> author of *The Marketing Imagination*

"Sell the sizzle, not the steak."
—Elmer Wheeler, U.S. sales speaker

"Sell the product of the product."
—Roger Von Oeck, U.S. creativity consultant

In other words, people don't buy drills, they buy holes. To help you decide what the benefits are of your product, idea or service, ask yourself these questions:

- What challenges does your product (idea or service) solve?
- What sizzle does it have? What do people talk about most after they use it?
- What is the *product* of the product?

When you must address a negative

Okay, I know. Sometimes, we need to disclose the negative side of something we're trying to promote—whether it's admitting to our spouse that we'll exceed our vacation budget if we book that fantastic cruise, or telling the boss that while we maintained budget we fell short of revenue goals, or advising a customer that he or she was denied credit.

"The aim of art is not to represent the outward appearance of things, but their inward significance."
—Aristotle

When I must tell someone a negative, I will tell them "I have great news and not-so-great news," always mentioning the great news first. Let's say I'm handed a report, asked to read it and then give my input. I have a few positive points and a few negative points. Exhibiting Enthusiasm and drawing on my can-do vocabulary, I present the positives first. "Mark, thank you for asking me for my input. I have a few comments and questions. First, I really liked the innovative concept and exciting delivery. I do have a few questions regarding the color of ink. I wonder what images that color calls to mind?" Putting the positive first softens the negative.

Imagine if I'd begun my response like this: "Mark, this color on this report is awful." He's not going to hear another word I say. What he will remember is that I was nasty and negative whether or not I was right.

Let's say a customer enters your company asking you if the particular car he or she wants comes in red. For this discussion, let's say the car does not come in red. What most people say is, "No, I'm sorry, it doesn't" (not even offering any alternatives). It is far more positive to say "That car comes in four fantastic colors—dolphin blue (sorry, I couldn't resist), gold, silver and black. I'd be happy to show them to you." What you really just said was, "No, it doesn't come in red, it comes in blue, gold, silver and black." But stating it in those terms throws two negatives at them—"no" and "doesn't." They often don't hear the rest.

Here's another example: A customer asks, "Can you deliver this to my house today?" Unfortunately, you don't have it and you can't get it delivered today. What are the first words that want to jump out of your mouth? "No, I can't do that. But I can do..." Remember, they stop listening after they hear the negative. Because you put a negative first, immediately, you have put this person on the defensive. Instead, just reverse the order. The first thing out of your mouth needs to be the positive. "I can call our downtown store and ask them to put you on their delivery schedule. We would be glad to have that for you the following day. Or would Wednesday be better?" (Note the positives.)

When the first thing a person hears is the solution to the problem, he or she is less likely to feel defensive. Often, he or she will not even realize there *is* a negative to the situation.

I remember hearing an example of someone who heard his doctor say "cancer," and heard nothing else. But the rest of the story was, "Cancer was suspected—and it was ruled out." However, the patient had stopped listening after that first negative word. Your customers do the same thing when you throw a negative in at the beginning of a sentence. So start with the positive!

Communicate Enthusiastically on the phone

It is just as important to be Enthusiastic and positive while on the phone. Conveying Enthusiasm over phone can be a bit more challenging because you are working without nonverbal messages that contribute to your dynamic impression.

Wherever you are—especially on the phone—use an Enthusiastic voice! Dolphins are one of the most Enthusiastic-sounding animals on earth—and one of the many reasons humans find them so endearing. Their clicks and whistles are captivating. Work on conveying your Enthusiasm through the phone whenever possible. Here are a few hints:

- Smile! It's hard to sound grumpy when you are smiling. Try it! Your smile will go right through to the customer and your customer will feel it and will respond more positively.
- You will sound friendly if you feel friendly. Again, look for things that you like about your customers and compliment them.
- Once you say hello, invite the caller to move forward with a statement such as "How may I help you today?"
- Be very courteous. Check out Letitia Baldrige's book, *Executive Manners*, and read up! Being polite goes a long way toward making a connection.
- Don't rush. It is very easy to fall into the habit of rushing over points that are familiar to you. But remember, this will all be new stuff to your listeners. Slow down in order to make a more dynamic connection.
- Change your body language to one of alertness and active interest—sit up, smile. You can always tell when the person on the other end is slouched down—it comes out in the voice.
- Make sure you have a friendly greeting. Identify yourself, and your company or department. Some great business phone greetings include:
  "Thank you for calling. This is Laura."
  "Thank you for choosing Executive Training Consultants. This is Laura."

- Enthusiastically thank everyone for calling your place of business when you begin and end your call. This starts and finishes the call by reinforcing how important and appreciated the customer is.
- Answer the phone in the first three rings. If the phone rings more than three times, customers can get the impression that you are too busy for them, or even think you are out of business (giving them reasons to check out your competition).
- Never eat while talking. If you think you can hide the fact that you are eating, drinking or chewing gum, *trust me*, you can't! If you really intend to make a dynamic connection, save the snacks for later.

Return your calls!

Unreturned phone calls make customers upset, and rightfully so. Reasons for unreturned calls vary: disorganization, avoidance or laziness. Whatever the reason, it's rude and creates very negative situations. As an owner, manager or salesperson, you need to think about ways to make sure calls are returned.

- Create a call-return system within your team that works!
- Consider clipboards or a designated pick-up area for messages.
- If you are a salesperson on the road, when you pick up your messages, write them down in your planner.
- Create a standard of returning phone calls the same day or by noon the next day if the call comes in too late.
- Pick up your voice mail messages daily and follow the guidelines listed here.

Transfers and holding

What are the two main areas of annoyance to you as a caller? I bet it's being transferred and being put on hold. How often is it happening in your business? I think if people really knew how frustrating those telephone mazes are today, they would change them immediately!

Have a friend of yours call your business and find a certain department. Don't give them any information an outside caller would not normally have. What do they hear? Is it the level of excellence you would hope your company portrays?

Whether you're the company owner or representative, here are some tips you can implement in order to convey excellence and customer service to those who call you:

- Never put someone on hold without asking! If you have to put someone on hold, ask for permission first and wait for an answer. If he or she says, "No, I really can't wait," maybe they have been on hold too long and called back in frustration. Maybe they really can't hold, and that's a person that needs to be assisted *now*.

- Offer the caller a choice: "May I transfer you to accounting, or may I take a message?" "May I put you on hold for a few moments, or may I take a message?"

- If you've had to put someone on hold, check back and thank the individual: "I appreciate your patience while holding."

- Use a customized message that your customers hear when they are placed on hold. Although you do not want customers to be placed on hold for very long, when they are, they are a captive audience. An Enthusiastic message or hold system that promotes your company, products or services is a great way to maximize on the moment.

- When you transfer someone, let them know the department and name of the individual of the person you are transferring them to.

Many people use call-waiting to avoid missing a phone call. However, call-waiting has no place in a business enviroment. Many businesses do not have enough phone lines. With multiple lines, when you are on the phone with one customer and another call is ringing and you cannot wrap up your present call quickly enough to get to the next customer in three rings—ask customers to hold—once only. Get the other line, quickly determining if you can assist the new customer instantly. If not, ask him or her to hold and finish up with the first customer quickly.

Voice mail can be useful if you are on another line, allowing you to carry on a conversation without interuption. However, because most people can't tell the difference between voice mail and answering machines, voice mail can be dangerous if it is used as a business sitter. When a business's main number is answered by voice mail, most people will perceive the business as small and possibly unable to handle their needs, and will be tempted to go elsewhere.

Maximize a valuable business asset: your voice

Whether talking on the phone, giving a speech, assisting customers on the showroom floor or making a presentation before a boss or a client, you will find that your voice is one of your most important—and most used—business tools. Treat it well and use it effectively. You get the best vocal projection when you stand up tall. This places your vocal chords, lungs and diaphragm in a position that can send your voice more easily across the room.

Developing and maintaining good, strong vocal production is like developing and maintaining a good strong heart—it takes exercise. Read the newspaper or, better yet, your actual presentation out loud prior to the formal presentation. Practice with a tape recorder to hear how your voice really sounds. Don't push or strain your voice. Allow it to be natural.

Your voice should have varied tones and inflections. This will make you sound more pleasant. When you practice, if what you are doing makes your voice tired or it hurts—stop doing it! Get a vocal coach, and see what you are doing wrong.

Voice self-critique

Performing a voice self-critique is crucial to understanding how you appear and sound to customers. I strongly recommend you tape yourself during phone conversations with customers. Simply place a tape recorder next to you while making outgoing calls. When you listen to the tape later, ask yourself these questions:

- **Tone.** Is your voice upbeat or monotonous? Do you sound enthusiastic or do you sound bored?

- **Speed.** Many salespeople speak too quickly at times simply because they are nervous or because they are so familiar with what they are saying. In one study I read, a receptionist spent more than one hour of an eight-hour workday repeating herself to callers simply because she spoke too rapidly for them to understand. Don't rush over points that are familiar to you—they probably aren't familiar to your caller.

- **Pitch.** How do you want to sound to your customer? Do you want to sound Enthusiastic, welcoming, appreciative, confident? Do you actually sound that way?

- **Volume.** Are you speaking at a comfortable volume level? Do you sound overpowering or do your customers need to strain to hear you?

- **Inflection.** Is your voice varied or subdued? Your voice should go up and down, just as any song does.

- **Clarity.** Are you slurring your words or are they clear and easy to understand?

- **Emotion.** Do you convey warmth and friendliness? Are you courteous?

Words and phrases to add Enthusiasm to your speech

By now, you probably have a good understanding of the many elements that go into conveying an Enthusiastic presence in your professional dealings. Indeed, while Enthusiasm must be genuine to be most effective, it is a trait that can—and should—be practiced and refined. You may feel uncomfortable at first, using unfamiliar gestures and language. But, trust me, this is not phony behavior. The words and gestures are merely tools that help unleash your genuine Enthusiasm. They'll soon feel natural. Following is a list of vocabulary and phrases that will help you convey your Enthusiasm effectively:

Dynamic words to add to your can-do vocabulary

100 percent	Extraordinary	Reliable
Absolutely!	Great	Resistant
Advanced	Guaranteed	Secure
Certainly!	Natural	Solid
Customized	Powerful	State-of-the-art
Cutting-edge	Preferred	Striking
Established	Premium	Superior
Excellent	Proven	Tremendous
Exceptional	Quality	Unique
Exclusive	Recommended	Yes!

Replace negative phrases with positive phrases

Don't say ...	**Do say ...**
"I'm sorry, there is nothing I can do."	"Let me find a way to fix this situation."
"Can I help you?"	"What can I help you find today?"
"Thank you for holding."	"Thank you for being patient, how can I help you?"
"We can't."	"We will."
"I'll try."	"I will."
"I don't know."	"I will find out."
"I'm sorry, that's all I can do."	"Please tell me, what else may I do?"

The Dolphin Dynamic

Don't say ...	Do say ...
"If we have those, they're on the shelf."	"Those should be on aisle four; I'm happy to show you."
"Would you mind calling back later?"	"Let me have your phone number. I'll have her call you back."
"Who's calling?"	"May I tell John who is calling?"
"May I speak with Mr. Smith please?"	"Good morning, may I speak with Bob Smith please? This is Laura Laaman returning his call."
"There's nobody here I can ask now."	"Let me have your phone number. We'll find that answer for you!"

"None are so old as those who have outlived enthusiasm."
—Henry David Thoreau

Quiz for the Enthusiastic Dynamic

1. Do you make a conscious effort to smile?
   ❏ Yes   ❏ No

2. Do you nod when speaking or listening to someone?
   ❏ Yes   ❏ No

3. Do you use open-handed gestures?
   ❏ Yes   ❏ No

4. Do you avoid folding your arms even when you're cold?
   ❏ Yes   ❏ No

5. Do you grab your customer's attention by using dynamic greetings?
   ❏ Yes   ❏ No

6. Do you make a point to sincerely compliment the people you are trying to connect with?
   ❏ Yes   ❏ No

7. Do you avoid negative people?
   ❏ Yes   ❏ No

8. Do you convey a can-do attitude (saying the positive first)?
   ❏ Yes   ❏ No

9. Do you introduce features and advantages and stress the *benefits* to your customers?
   ❏ Yes   ❏ No

10. Do you practice using dynamic words?
    ❏ Yes   ❏ No

11. Do you return your phone calls promptly?
    ❏ Yes   ❏ No

12. Have you tape-recorded your voice in order to hear and improve your speech?
     ❏ Yes   ❏ No

13. Do you avoid putting your hands in your pockets?
     ❏ Yes   ❏ No

14. Do you come out from behind your desk or the counter when communicating with people?
     ❏ Yes   ❏ No

15. Do you use your customers' names when addressing them?
     ❏ Yes   ❏ No

16. Do you always shake someone's hand when you introduce yourself?
     ❏ Yes   ❏ No

17. Do you look for common ground with your customers?
     ❏ Yes   ❏ No

18. Do you avoid using slang or technical language in your conversations?
     ❏ Yes   ❏ No

19. When a problem—or rather, situation—arises, do you take the steps necessary to resolve it, even if it's not your responsibility?
     ❏ Yes   ❏ No

20. Are you able to be positive about your product, even when discussing a negative?
     ❏ Yes   ❏ No

If you answered 18 to 20 yes's, you exhibit a high degree of dolphin-like Enthusiasm and will increase your success rapidly.

If you answered 13 to 17 yes's, beware—sharks are in the water with you.

If you answered 10 to 12 yes's, you are wounded and sharks are moving in.

If you answered nine or less yes's, *get out of the water*—you are about to be eaten alive!

Checklist for the Enthusiastic Dynamic

• First and foremost—smile!

• Use dynamic gestures and words that communicate Enthusiasm.

• Continually ask yourself, "How do I look to the person across from me?"

• Go out of your way to exceed your customer's expectations.

• Think about your vocabulary—substitute dynamic and positive words for slang, technical or wishy-washy language.

• Be sure to establish and maintain positive eye contact.

• Use open-ended gestures to nonverbally reinforce your honesty and your credibility.

• Be sure to learn your customer's name—and use it.

• Develop an effective handshake—firm, yet personal.

• Sincerely compliment the people you are trying to connect with.

• Act and sound Enthusiastic—all the time!

• Stress how your product or service will benefit your customer, citing features, advantages and benefits of your product or service.

• Tell your customers what you *can* do, not what you can't.

• When asked how you are, respond with, "Great," "Terrific" or "Excellent" even when you don't feel that way.

• When you begin to feel uncomfortable with increased Enthusiasm, know that you are setting yourself apart from others and are on your way to becoming more successful.

• Develop an effective and dynamic greeting for your customers.

• If co-workers have the disease of negativism, try to cure them. If you can't cure them, avoid their disease.

• Learn to view "problems" as "situations" or "challenges"—and to respond to others' "problems" in the same way.

• If you *have* to deal with negatives, be sure to couch them in positive language.

In conclusion about Enthusiasm

We learn a great deal from dolphins about Enthusiasm, as well as Determination, Instinct and Vision. Their perpetual smiles, clicks, whistles and movements are a fanfare of Enthusiasm. Yours should be as well.

Enthusiasm will set you apart from the competition and make your journey much more enjoyable. When you are working hard, tuned in to those around you and focusing on your goals, Enthusiasm helps other people become attracted to you. People are drawn to Enthusiastic people and businesses like magnets!

Enthusiasm is not for the weak but for the strong and successful. Others may look at you strangely for being so Enthusiastic. Great! You can laugh all the way to the bank. There is a direct correlation between Enthusiasm and success. I hope you will employ this powerful strategy immediately. It will provide a fabulous foundation for you and for those around you. Don't let any mean nasty sharks take a bite out of your Enthusiasm.

Conclusion:
Make a Splash!

No professional in today's shark-infested business waters should be without the skills covered in this book. When you employ Determination, Instinct, Vision and Enthusiasm, and just start moving, the dynamics of this formula will, without fail, pull you toward your goals. The *Determination* will push you. Your *Instinct* will help you work with people. The *Vision* will keep you on track and the *Enthusiasm* will make the journey more enjoyable—both for you and for those around you.

Your talents are a gift. These talents can produce many positive, meaningful results. You should continually strive to enhance these talents for great personal and professional growth. However, the more talented you are, the more opportunity you have to misuse your gift. Sharks and fools misuse their talents, not dolphins! Use your talents to help yourself as well as those around you.

Recently, a pilot whale and its calf wandered too close to shore and became disoriented. It became obvious that the whale could not find its way back to deeper, safer waters without assistance. Onlookers watched for days as the mother whale became increasingly frantic and weaker. It was as if the mother whale knew she must stay alert to protect her young calf. Sensing her weakened condition, sharks moved in to attack the calf. Just as the sharks came closer, the whales' protectors arrived! No, not the Coast Guard—a pod of dolphins. They moved in, circling the mother and her young calf. Amazingly, trustingly, the whale seemed to relax and rest.

The dolphins stayed with the pair for more than two days. Eventually, the Coast Guard arrived and helped the pod of dolphins guide the mother whale and her calf back to safety. The dolphins used their skills to help the whales—as they have helped fishermen and shipwreck victims countless times before.

The Dolphin Dynamic

Just as these dolphins utilize their unique skills to protect and guide the whales to safer waters, today's successful businesspeople tap into their talents—not just for their own gain, but to help others as well. Whether promoting the financial health of their company, mentoring a less-experienced employee or contributing time and expertise to a charitable cause, dynamic professionals know the value and importance of sharing their talents for the betterment of others.

Bring the Dolphin Dynamic
to Your Organization —
and *Make a Splash!*

Professional training and speaking

If you are interested in helping the individuals in your organization become more Determined, Instinctive, Vision-oriented and Enthusiastic, call my office for training or speaking information.

All of our training courses are customized exclusively with your company in mind. Some of the many courses we offer are:

- Sales training.
- Customer focus training.
- Leadership training.
- Time management.
- Stress management.

Each course is designed to help your business reach its goals.

Call today to fulfill your training needs.
1-800-TRAINING
872 - 4646

Dive with the dolphins!

*Personal and professional development seminars
with Laura and the dolphins.*

*Paradise locations include the Florida Keys,
Bahamas and Hawaii.*

Prices for the Dolphin Destinations, including seminars and actual
dolphin interaction, start at only $995 (for three days per person based on
double occupancy).

Contact our office for details.
1-800-872-4646

The Dolphin Department

Call 1-800-872-4646 today to order our
popular dolphin specialty items!

Dexter the dolphin

Our furry stuffed dolphin produces
realistic clicks and whistles. A
wonderful gift for dolphin lovers of all
ages. This lovable creature is 13" nose to
tail and 6" from fin to fin. $14.95.

Stress-relieving dolphin music

Sounds of the dolphins and the gentle ocean will relax you.
Specify cassette ($8.95) or CD ($9.95).

Stress-relieving dolphin squeezee

A dolphin that you can take your
frustrations out on—and it always
looks adorable. $8.95.

DIVE into Success!

This bimonthly newsletter provides you with powerful and
practical information that will inspire and motivate the sales,
management and customer service professionals in your
organization. Annual fee is $29.95.

All orders over $20 receive a high-quality dolphin gift.
Call 1-800-872-4646 to order. MasterCard and Visa accepted.
Small shipping and handling fees. Please call for exact charges.

Suggested Reading

If you would like additional information on manners, I am confident that you will find Letitia Baldrige's book, *The Complete Guide to Executive Manners*, enlightening and entertaining.

For further information on handwriting analysis, I recommend Ann Mahony's book, *Handwriting & Personality, How Graphology Reveals What Makes People Tick*.

For another book to increase your selling ability, I recommend *How to Master the Art of Selling*, by Tom Hopkins.

Success Magazine can provide you with motivation and in-depth insight into the minds and techniques of proven successful individuals.

And for information on the world of professional speaking—books, videos and audio albums—contact Lilly Walters or Dottie Walters at The Walters International Speakers Bureau, P.O. Box 1120, Glendora, CA, 91740; 818-335-8069, fax 818-335-6127.

Index

Activity charts, 143-146
Adapting your style to
others, 93-95
Addressing a negative, 198-199
Agreement, confirming, 117-118
Anatomy of an Illness, 186
Appearance, 41-53
Ash, Mary Kay, 114
Assumptive vocabulary,
power of, 141, 151
Attitude, 53-57

Baldrige, Letitia, 48, 174-176, 200
Bar charts, 142
Believing in yourself, 55
Benefits, of your product, 196-198
Body language, 23, 164-172, 200
observing, 71-81
Brains-plus-brawn approach, 24
Brawn-plus-brains approach, 21
Breaks, rest, 32
Briefcase, carrying, 42, 45, 50
Business cards, 49, 53
Business environment, 48-49

Calendar, using, 26-27
Can-do attitude, 53-55, 59
Can-do vocabulary, 186-188,
204-206
Car wait time, using, 31
Car, appearance of, 50
Career Profile Assessments, 95-96

Checklist
for the Determined
Dynamic, 65-66
for the Enthusiastic
Dynamic, 209
for the Instinctive
Dynamic, 132-133
for the Vision Dynamic, 161
Closed-ended questions, 110-111
Clothes, 44-47, 50-53
Clutter, removing, 28
Commitment signals,
reading, 116-117
Common ground,
establishing, 182-183
Complimenting, to make
connections, 180-182
Confidence, 53-55
Connection
dolphin, 13-14
mind-body, 57-58
with customers, 15-18
Connections, establishing, 179-185
Contests and incentives, 151-154
Customer, dissatisfied, 122-123
Customer focus quiz, 172
Customer service, 172-173
Customers' participation,
rewarding, 106, 108

Delegating, 26, 30-31
Determination, 10ff, 19-67

Determined personality,
  86-87, 93-95
Difficult people, dealing with, 118
Disciplining employees, 126-128
Dissatisfied customer, 122-123
Dolphin Research Center
  (DRC), 10, 15, 25, 35, 78,
  83, 136, 184
Dolphin Therapy, 13-14, 18
Dorsal pull, 14-15
Dress-down days, 46
Drowned and the Saved, 158
Dynamic Four, 163-210
Dynamic One, 19-67
Dynamic Three, 135-162
Dynamic Two, 69-134

E-mail, 32
Eating in front of others, 44
Echolocation, 70
Effort, 21-23
Emotional encounters,
  diffusing, 119-122
Employees
  disciplining, 126-128
  hiring, 123-126
  terminating, 128-129
Enthusiasm, 10ff, 163-210
  spreading, 186-187
Enthusiastic Dynamic
  checklist for, 209
  quiz for, 207-208
Enthusiastic personality, 91-93
Environment
  business, 48-49
  unenthusiastic, 185-186
Ethic, work, 19-22
Executive Manners, 48, 200
Exercise, 57-58

Expectation, law of, 150-151
Expectations, exceeding, 172-173
Exploration, 81-85
Eye contact, 167

Features, of your product, 196-198
Feedback, from customers,
  101-114
Feel, felt, found technique, 37, 121
Filing, 28
Firing employees, 128-129
Focusing your Vision, 136
Folded arms, 170
Following up, 37-41, 122, 146

Gestures
  Enthusiastic, 164-170
  to avoid, 170-172
Getting the most out of
  your day, 25-26
Goal charts, 139-146
Goals, setting, 26, 136ff
Graphology, 97-99
Great-attitude people, 55-57
Greetings
  attention-grabbing, 173-178,
    188-189, 200
  insincere, 178
  practicing while busy, 179
Gum, chewing, 43-44

Handshakes, powerful, 174-176
Handwriting analysis, 97-99
Hiding behind barriers, 171
Hill, Napoleon, 19, 157
Hiring employees, 123-126
Holding phone calls, 201-202
Home, balancing with work, 61-62
Hopkins, Tom, 190

Humor, to make
   connections, 184-185
Hygiene, personal, 43

Image
   enhancing, 41-53
   positive, 166-170
In-line wait time, using, 31
Incentives and contests, 151-154
Individual needs,
   addressing, 114-116
Insecurity, 16
Instinct, 10ff, 69-134
Instinctive Dynamic
   checklist for, 132-133
   quiz for, 130-131
Instinctive
   personality, 87-89, 92-94
Internal customer survey,
   sample, 107
Internal talk, positive, 150-151
Interruptions, 26, 29
Interviewing potential
   employees, 124-126

Job satisfaction, 25

Kinko's Copies, 56-57

Language
   nontechnical, 195
   "soft," 193-194
Leading, 81
Learning, 60-61
Leisure time, enjoying, 26, 32-33
Likability, 183-184
Loneliness at the top, 62

Management, 123-129

Manners, 48, 53
Marketing Imagination, 197
Materials, presentation, 49-50
Mehrabian, Albert, 84, 165
Mekota, Mark, 153-154
Memorization, 23
Mental possession, 147-150
Mind-body connection, 57-58
Mirroring and modeling, 100
Monitoring your progress, 147
Motivation, 13, 18

Nathanson, David E.,
   Ph.D., 14, 18
Negative, addressing a, 198-199
Negative silent signals, 74-75
Negative situations, changing to
   positive, 190-191
Networking, 22
Nodding, 167
Nonverbal message, 164-172
Nutrition, 58

Objections, overcoming, 33-37
Obstacles, overcoming, 19, 33-34
101 Simple Things to Grow Your
   Business and Yourself, 31
Open-ended questions, 111-113
Open-handed gestures, 168-169
Openers,
   attention-grabbing, 176-178

Pace
   adjusting, 79-81
   matching, 78-79
Perception, intuitive, 69-81
Persistence, 19
Personality styles,
   exploring, 83-95

Phone, being positive
on the, 200-204
Phone calls, follow-up, 40-41, 146
Phone wait time, using, 31
Planner, using, 26-27
Planning, lack of, 26
Positive silent signals, 76
Posting goals, 139ff
Practice, 22-24
Preparation, 22-24
Prescription without
examination, 81-82
Presentation materials, 49-50
Prioritizing, 26-28
Procrastination, 26-28
Product, features and
benefits, 196-198
Productivity, 25
Professional sonar, 69-70
Profits, 25
Prospecting, 22
Protected territories, working
within, 73, 77

Questioning, 81-85
Questions
asking customers, 101-114
hiring, 124-125
Quiet time, scheduling, 26, 30
Quiz
for the Determined
Dynamic, 63-64
for the Enthusiastic
Dynamic, 207-208
for the Instinctive
Dynamic, 130-131
for the Vision Dynamic, 159-160
Rapport, establishing, 120-121
Recall strategy, 37

Reception areas, company, 49
Referrals, 146
Reilly, Steve, 56-57
Rejection, 59
Relations, interpersonal, 25
Researching, 81-85
Resilience, 59
Returning phone calls, 201
Reward, for achieved goal, 141
Role-playing, 12, 23-24, 41

Safety zones, 73, 77
Sales contests, 151-154
Sarcasm, avoiding, 185
Satisfaction, job, 25
Secrets, survey, 106
Service, customer, 172-173
Shaping, 106, 108, 137-138, 187
Signals, reading silent, 69-81
Skills
greeting, 173-178, 188-189, 200
listening and
questioning, 108-109
Sleep, adequate, 58
Smiling, 166-167, 200
Smoking, 43-44
"Soft" language, 193-194
Solution, creating, 121-122
Sonar, professional, 69-70
Star boards, 147
Stationing, 136
Strategies, planning, 27
Success, 12-13
Survey card, 38-40
Surveys, customer, 101-114

Team shirts, 50-51
Telephone survey,
sample, 104-105

Terminating employees, 128-129
Thank-you notes, 144-145
Think & Grow Rich, 19, 157
Thoreau, Henry David, 158, 206
Time, using wisely, 25-33
Tools of your trade, 48-50, 53
Touching, 169-170
Transferring phone calls, 201-202

Unenthusiastic environment,
  coping with, 185-186
Uniforms, 50-51
UPS, 45

Vanderbilt, Amy, 48
Verbal communication, 165
Vision, 10ff, 135-162
Vision Dynamic
  checklist for, 161
  quiz for, 159-160
Visionary personality, 89-93
Visual exploration, 82-83

Visualization, 138-139
Vocabulary
  can-do, 186-188, 204-206
  wishy-washy, 193-194
Vocal communication, 165
Voice, as a business asset, 203-204

Wait times, using
  effectively, 26,31-32
Walters, Dottie, 21, 31, 33,
  113, 119
Walters, Lilly, 32
Watch-checking, 171
Wegmans, 46-47
*What Your First Grader
  Needs to Know*, 20
Work ethic, 19-22, 61-62
Worrying, 26
Writing down tasks, 139ff

Ziglar, Zig, 56